HARRIET TUBMAN

HARRIET TUBMAN

M.W. Taylor

Senior Consulting Editor
Nathan Irvin Huggins
Director
W.E.B. Du Bois Institute for Afro-American Research
Harvard University

GROLIER INCORPORATED
Danbury, Connecticut

Editor-in-Chief   Remmel Nunn
Managing Editor   Karyn Gullen Browne
Copy Chief   Juliann Barbato
Picture Editor   Adrian G. Allen
Art Director   Maria Epes
Deputy Copy Chief   Mark Rifkin
Assistant Art Director   Loraine Machlin
Manufacturing Manager   Gerald Levine
Systems Manager   Rachel Vigier
Production Manager   Joseph Romano
Production Coordinator   Marie Claire Cebrián

Black Americans of Achievement
Senior Editor   Richard Rennert

Staff for HARRIET TUBMAN
Copy Editor   Philip Koslow
Editorial Assistant   Leigh Hope Wood
Picture Researcher   Nisa Rauschenberg
Designer   Ghila Krajzman
Cover Illustration   Vilma Ortiz

**This edition published
exclusively for the
Amway Corporation.**

ISBN 0-7172 8556-1

Frontispiece: *Harriet Tubman
(far left) poses with a group of
former slaves in the North.*

CONTENTS

ON
ACHIEVEMENT

———————— ❧ ————————

Coretta Scott King

Before you begin this book, I hope you will ask yourself what the word excellence means to you. I think that it's a question we should all ask, and keep asking as we grow older and change. Because the truest answer to it should never change. When you think of excellence, perhaps you think of success at work; or of becoming wealthy; or meeting the right person, getting married, and having a good family life.

Those important goals are worth striving for, but there is a better way to look at excellence. As Martin Luther King, Jr., said in one of his last sermons, "I want you to be first in love. I want you to be first in moral excellence. I want you to be first in generosity. If you want to be important, wonderful. If you want to be great, wonderful. But recognize that he who is greatest among you shall be your servant."

My husband, Martin Luther King, Jr., knew that the true meaning of achievement is service. When I met him, in 1952, he was already ordained as a Baptist preacher and was working towards a doctoral degree at Boston University. I was studying at the New England Conservatory and dreamed of accomplishments in music. We married a year later, and after I graduated the following year we moved to Montgomery, Alabama. We didn't know it then, but our notions of achievement were about to undergo a dramatic change.

You may have read or heard about what happened next. What began with the boycott of a local bus line grew into a national movement, and by the time he was assassinated in 1968 my husband had fashioned a black movement powerful enough to shatter forever the practice of racial segregation. What you may not have read about is where he got his method for resisting injustice without compromising his religious beliefs.

He adopted the strategy of nonviolence from a man of a different race, who lived in a distant country, and even practiced a different religion. The man was Mahatma Gandhi, the great leader of India, who devoted his life to serving humanity in the spirit of love and nonviolence. It was in these principles that Martin discovered his method for social reform. More than anything else, those two principles were the key to his achievements.

This book is about black Americans who served society through the excellence of their achievements. It forms a part of the rich history of black men and women in America—a history of stunning accomplishments in every field of human endeavor, from literature and art to science, industry, education, diplomacy, athletics, jurisprudence, even polar exploration.

Not all of the people in this history had the same ideals, but I think you will find something that all of them have in common. Like Martin Luther King, Jr., they all decided to become "drum majors" and serve humanity. In that principle—whether it was expressed in books, inventions, or song—they found something outside themselves to use as a goal and a guide. Something that showed them a way to serve others, instead of living only for themselves.

Reading the stories of these courageous men and women not only helps us discover the principles that we will use to guide our own lives but also teaches us about our black heritage and about America itself. It is crucial for us to know the heroes and heroines of our history and to realize that the price we paid in our struggle for equality in America was dear. But we must also understand that we have gotten as far as we have partly because America's democratic system and ideals made it possible.

We are still struggling with racism and prejudice. But the great men and women in this series are a tribute to the spirit of our democratic ideals and the system in which they have flourished. And that makes their stories special and worth knowing. ✥

HARRIET TUBMAN

1

A WOMAN
CALLED MOSES

❧

ON THE AFTERNOON of April 27, 1860, a tall black man named Charles Nalle stood defiantly before United States Commissioner Miles Beach in a courthouse in Troy, New York. A runaway slave, Nalle was being watched closely by an assortment of attorneys, court officers, and armed U.S. marshals, as well as Henry J. Wall, a plantation agent from Virginia. The marshals and Wall had just finished giving evidence against Nalle in their effort to send him back into slavery. Two years earlier, he had escaped from Virginia and made his way north to freedom.

But on this spring afternoon, 500 miles from the nearest slave state, Nalle faced the prospect of being told he was still a slave. According to the Fugitive Slave Act, federal legislation that was passed in 1850, he remained the property of his owner, even in a free state. The U.S. government was legally obliged to return a captured slave to bondage.

As the sounds of a crowd gathering outside the courthouse began to fill the second-floor room, Commissioner Beach disclosed his chilling decision to the court: Nalle must be turned over to Wall and returned to his southern master. Nalle edged toward the window. Below, on First and State streets, their eyes fixed on him, stood more than 1,000 people, black and white, women and men. Nalle knew that Troy, like most other northern cities, was home to many opponents of slavery. Some of these abolitionists favored ending slavery peacefully and lawfully. Others were ready and willing to help a slave escape any way they could.

Nalle lunged for the window. He almost made it through, but marshals seized his arms and dragged him back into the courtroom. At that moment, freedom must have seemed like a dream to Nalle. Even if the people outside the courthouse had wanted to come to his aid, how could they do it? He was now closely guarded by armed men, and he had no friends or allies nearby. The only black face in sight belonged to a spectator, a bent old woman wearing a shawl and bonnet and carrying a basket. The guards had probably let her in because they felt sorry for her. What could one old woman do, anyway?

A band of patrollers—white slave catchers—guns down a quartet of fleeing blacks in the mid-1800s. The passage of the Fugitive Slave Act in 1850 accelerated the South's relentless tracking of runaways.

Suddenly, a voice from the crowd below shouted a question that was heard in the courtroom: How much money would it take for the southern agent to free Nalle?

"Twelve hundred dollars," Wall replied.

Purses were opened and hats hastily passed. A few minutes later, the spectators announced that they had collected the price of Charles Nalle's freedom. Agent Wall responded by raising the figure to $1,500. A low, angry roar swept the crowd: The slave catcher was mocking them; he had no intention of releasing Nalle.

The abolitionists had tried to save Nalle and had failed. There was nothing else they could do. Now that the hearing was over, he would be put aboard a train and sent south, back into slavery.

Guards chained Nalle's hands and pushed him toward the stairs that led to the street. Near the landing, the guards brushed aside the old black woman, who was standing quietly, her head bowed. But as soon as they had passed her, she tore off her sunbonnet and raced to the window. "Here he comes," she shouted to the people below. "Take him!"

The crowd surged forward, meeting Nalle and his guards at the foot of the stairs. The marshals raised their clubs, yet the crowd continued to press in. Then down the stairs, like an avenging angel, charged the "old woman." Without her shawl, basket, and stooped pose, she revealed herself as a small, very dark-skinned woman of about 40. Her eyes were bright, even fierce; her arms were muscular, her fists clenched. The marshals ducked as she flew at them, punching furiously and shouting at the top of her lungs.

"Drag him to the river!" the woman cried. "Drown him! But don't let them have him!" Then, an eyewitness reported later, "like a wildcat" she

knocked down one of Nalle's guards and wrapped her arms around the manacled prisoner. Wrenching him away from a second guard, she pulled Nalle through the crowd toward the river. Marshals flailed at Nalle and his rescuer with fists and clubs, but the woman refused to let go. The crowd joined her.

The *Troy Whig* described the scene as "a regular battlefield." In the "surging mass" of people, said the newspaper, "the pulling, hauling, mauling, and shouting gave evidences of frantic efforts on the part of the rescuers, and a stern resistance from the conservators of the law." The street filled with screams, curses, and the smell of gunpowder.

"In the melee," a local attorney stated later, the small black woman "was repeatedly beaten over the

Slaves—men, women, and children—carry their harvest after a 16-hour day in the cotton fields. Escaping from such bondage in 1858, Virginian Charles Nalle was recaptured two years later in Troy, New York, but was eventually freed by Tubman and others.

head with policemen's clubs, but she never for a moment released her hold, but cheered Nalle and his friends with her voice, and struggled with the officers until they were literally worn out with their exertions, and Nalle was separated from them. True she had strong and earnest helpers in her struggle, some of whom had white faces as well as human hearts, and are now in Heaven. But she exposed herself to the fury of the sympathizers with slavery without fear, and suffered their blows without flinching."

Finally, the crowd managed to pull Nalle, chains and all, away from his captors. They rushed the bleeding, dazed fugitive to the riverbank and pushed him onto a waiting rowboat. As an oarsman pulled away from the shore, the black woman, along with some

400 allies, boarded a steam-powered ferryboat and followed the rowboat.

But more marshals, alerted by telegraph, awaited them across the river. They seized Nalle, locked him in a house, and placed armed guards at every window. Undeterred, the woman and her friends began to hurl rocks at the makeshift jail. The marshals responded with gunfire, and the crowd fell back. Then a man's voice shouted, "Who cares? They can only kill a dozen of us—come on!"

Eager to do his part, a huge black man emerged from the crowd, strode up to the house, and kicked down the door. Marshals swiftly felled him with an ax, but his body jammed the door open, and the abolitionists poured through. Strong hands picked up the battered Nalle, carried him outside, and put him into a wagon that rolled north, carrying the former slave toward Canada and freedom. Meanwhile, the crowd dispersed, and the black woman disappeared from view.

When the liberated slave revived, he asked about the woman who had engineered his rescue. Nalle's

A photographer in the mid-1800s created this powerful image of a slave on the run. In 1850 alone, more than 1,000 blacks fled their southern plantations for the free states of the North.

$100
REWARD.

Ran away from my farm, near Buena Vista P. O., Prince George's County, Maryland, on the first day of April, 1855, my servant MATHEW TURNER.

He is about five feet six or eight inches high; weighs from one hundred and sixty to one hundred and eighty pounds; he is very black, and has a remarkably thick upper lip and neck; looks as if his eyes are half closed; walks slow, and talks and laughs loud.

I will give One Hundred Dollars reward to whoever will secure him in jail, so that I get him again, no matter where taken.

MARCUS DU VAL.

BUENA VISTA P. O., MD.,
MAY 10, 1855.

Posted by a Maryland slave owner in 1855, a handbill offers $100 for the return of "servant" Mathew Turner. Notices about runaways, increasingly common in the decade before the Civil War, inspired widespread manhunts.

escorts told him she had gone into hiding because she carried a price on her head—she was wanted by authorities in both the North and the South for helping slaves escape from their masters. Her name was Harriet Tubman, they said, but she was better known as "Moses." A namesake of the biblical prophet who had brought his people out of bondage and into the Promised Land, Tubman had led more of her brethren out of Egypt—as she called the slaveholding South— than any other person, black or white, male or female, in American history. ✤

2

THE SHORT CHILDHOOD OF A SLAVE

HARRIET TUBMAN WAS born into slavery as Harriet Ross around 1820 on the Eastern Shore, a peninsula shared by the state of Delaware and parts of Maryland and Virginia. Bordered on the east by the Atlantic Ocean and on the west by the shallow, fish-filled waters of Chesapeake Bay, the area has a moderate climate. The Eastern Shore's flat, rich farmland is also known as the Tidewater because its countless inlets, swamps, and small rivers rise and fall with the tides of the nearby sea. Near the center of the peninsula, where Delaware and Maryland meet, is the nation's northernmost cypress swamp.

Although the Eastern Shore lies only a few miles from the industrial cities of Baltimore and Philadelphia, its atmosphere resembles that of the Deep South. Situated at the Confederacy's northernmost edge, it was the birthplace of some of the most renowned and valiant warriors in the battle against slavery, including Frederick Douglass and the woman who would be known as Moses.

Harriet Ross's birthdate is approximate because no one officially recorded it; few slaves could read or write, and slave owners kept no more precise data on

Facing a camera in the mid-1800s, a young slave embraces his little brother protectively. Tubman, like most children born into slavery, started work early; she was five years old when her master hired her out as a housemaid.

19

A southern planter barks out a command to his field slaves. As an adult, Tubman said of her cruel masters: "They didn't know any better. . . . They were brought up with the whip in their hand."

the lives of their slaves than they did on the lives of their pigs and chickens. Harriet was one of 11 children born to Harriet Green and Benjamin Ross, slaves belonging to Maryland planter Edward Brodas. Harriet's mother, known as Old Rit, gave her daughter the "cradle name" of Araminta. The little girl's family usually called her Minty.

Both Green and Ross were full-blooded Africans; their parents had been brought to the United States in chains. According to legend, the family came from the Ashanti, a West African warrior people who successfully battled the British during much of the 19th century. Harriet Tubman believed in this version of her roots; as an adult, she sometimes remarked that she was "one of those Ashantis." In any case, she would prove to be a formidable warrior herself.

On his plantation, situated on the Big Buckwater River in the Tidewater's Dorchester County, Edward

Brodas raised apples, wheat, rye, and corn. His land also included vast stands of trees, including oak, cypress, and poplar, which he sold to the Baltimore shipyards across the Chesapeake Bay. Harriet's father, Benjamin ("Old Ben") Ross, spent most of his days cutting timber for his master. Harriet's mother worked for the Brodas family in their elegant home, called "the big house" by the slaves.

Like many slave owners in the Upper South, Edward Brodas bred and raised blacks as a cash crop, renting and selling them to others. Georgia slave traders made frequent appearances in the neighborhood; by the time she was 13, Harriet Ross had seen sisters, brothers, and friends sold "down the river" to work on the vast cotton and sugar plantations of the Deep South.

The childhood of a slave was short. When Harriet was five years old, her master rented her to a local couple named Cook. At their home, the little girl slept on the kitchen floor, poking her feet under the fireplace ashes when the nights grew cold. For meals, she shared table scraps with the Cooks' dogs.

Mrs. Cook put Harriet to work winding yarn, but when the young slave proved slow at the job, her mistress turned her over to her husband. He assigned Harriet to watch his muskrat traps. Now she spent her days, barefoot and wearing only a thin shirt, wading in the edge of the icy river, looking for animals on James Cook's traplines. Before long, she developed a cough and a high fever, which her masters accused her of faking to escape work. Calling her useless, lazy, and stupid, the Cooks finally sent her back to the Brodas plantation. There, under her mother's care, Harriet recovered from a six-week bout of measles and bronchitis. Then Brodas rented her again, this time to a woman who wanted a housekeeper and baby nurse.

Many years after the experience, Harriet Tubman described it to a friend who recorded her account:

I was only seven years old when I was sent away to take care of a baby. I was so little that I had to sit on the floor and have the baby put on my lap. And that baby was always on my lap except when it was asleep or its mother was feeding it.

One morning, after breakfast, she had the baby, and I stood by the table waiting until I was to take it; near me was a bowl of lumps of white sugar. My mistress got into a great quarrel with her husband; she had an awful temper, and she would scold and storm and call him all kinds of names.

Now, you know, I never had anything good, no sweet, no sugar; and that sugar, right by me, did look so nice, and my mistress's back was turned to me while she was fighting with her husband, so I just put my fingers in the sugar bowl to take one lump and maybe she heard me for she turned and saw me.

The next minute she had the rawhide down. I gave one jump out of the door and I saw that they came after me, but I just flew and they didn't catch me. I ran and I ran and I passed many a house, but I didn't dare to stop for they all knew my mistress and they would send me back.

By and by when I was almost tuckered out, I came to a great big pigpen. There was an old sow there, and perhaps eight or ten little pigs. I tumbled over [the fence] and fell in . . . so beaten out that I could not stir.

And I stayed there from Friday until the next Tuesday, fighting with those little pigs for the potato peelings and the other scraps that came down in the trough. The old sow would push me away when I tried to get her children's food, and I was awfully afraid of her. By Tuesday I was so starved I knew I had to go back to my mistress. I didn't have anywhere else to go, even though I knew what was coming. So I went back.

The terrified little girl returned to her mistress, who gave her a savage whipping, then brought her back to the Brodas plantation. Harriet, said the woman who had rented her, "wasn't worth a sixpence." Once again, Old Rit nursed her child, salving the fresh wounds that overlay the scars from earlier beatings. And once again, as soon as Harriet was able to work, Brodas hired her out. This time, she was put to work splitting fence rails and loading timber on wagons. It was backbreaking labor, better suited to a brawny adult male than a little girl. Nevertheless, Harriet preferred it, she said later, to working in a house under the harsh scrutiny of a "lady."

By the time she was in her early teens, Harriet was known as a strong but surly laborer, unfit for indoor work but useful as a field hand. She never forgot her painful childhood, and she never had a good word for any of her masters. If they had any excuse for their cruelty, she asserted, it was ignorance. "They didn't know any better. It's the way they were brought up . . . with the whip in their hand," she said as an adult. "Now that wasn't the way on all plantations," she added. "There were good masters and mistresses, as I've heard tell. But I didn't happen to come across any of them."

In 1831, when Harriet was about 11, exciting but terrifying rumors swept the slave quarters of the Brodas estate. Nat Turner, a slave on a Virginia plantation—only 100 miles away, across the Chesapeake Bay—had led an army of 60 rebel slaves against their white masters. More than 50 whites, whispered the Brodas slaves to one another, had been killed in the uprising. True, Turner and his men had lost their battle, but their daring revolt offered proof that Africans were men, not animals, and that they would fight and die for their freedom.

Turner's was not the only black uprising in the 19th-century South. In 1800, a Virginia slave named Gabriel Prosser had tried and failed to establish an independent black state, and in 1822, Denmark Vesey had organized hundreds of blacks in a spectacular but futile bid for freedom in South Carolina. These rebellions sparked hope and elation among the South's blacks, terror among its whites.

Slaves found other ways, too, to establish some degree of independence. Some pretended to be stupid, "accidentally" destroying their masters' tools and

Nat Turner, the Virginia slave who led a revolt in 1831, surrenders after evading pursuers for two months. News of Turner's rebellion, in which more than 50 whites were killed, sent waves of fear—and pride—through the Brodas plantation's slaves.

Labeled like cattle, most slaves wore tags showing the name of their master. Free blacks carried medallions marked with the liberty cap (top), a token given to freed slaves in ancient Rome.

crops; others ran away when they saw their chance. Escape, however, was extremely difficult. When a planter reported a runaway slave, bands of mounted white men, known as patrollers ("patterollers" to the slave community), ranged through the countryside, tracking the fugitives with dogs. The standard punishment for runaways was whipping, branding with the letter *R*, and exile to the Deep South, where working conditions for slaves were more brutal than anywhere else. The slaves who trudged off in chains to Louisiana or Georgia never came back and rarely lived long.

During Harriet's childhood, even runaway slaves who managed to elude their pursuers had no place to go. Not until the mid-19th century, when the abolitionist movement began to develop in the North, was there any refuge for blacks fleeing their bonds.

It was an escaping slave who inadvertently brought disaster to 15-year-old Harriet. In the fall of 1835, she was shucking corn along with the rest of the plantation's workers when she noticed a tall black man sneaking away from the group. The overseer, carrying his snakeskin whip as usual, followed the black man. So did Harriet.

Catching up with the runaway at the crossroads store, the overseer prepared to whip him. He spotted Harriet and told her to hold the slave while he tied him up for the lashing. She refused. The black man bolted, and Harriet stationed herself in the doorway, blocking the overseer's way. Enraged, he grabbed a two-pound lead weight from the store counter and flung it after the running slave. The weight missed its mark and hit Harriet squarely in the head. She fell like a stone, blood pouring from a deep gash in her forehead.

When Harriet was carried home, her shocked mother dressed the wound, stopped the bleeding, and prayed. But the teenager remained in a coma for weeks, lying on a bed of rags in the corner of her family's windowless wooden cabin. Not until the following spring was she able to get up and walk unaided. Although her injury was never medically diagnosed (doctors were rarely wasted on slaves), Harriet had probably suffered a fractured skull and severe concussion.

She would carry a scar and a dent in her forehead for the rest of her life and, from that point on, would suffer periodic "sleeping fits." Without warning, wherever she might be, she would suddenly fall into a deep sleep. Such attacks took place as often as three or four times a day, even when Harriet was in the middle of a conversation. Until she regained consciousness by herself, nothing could rouse her.

While Harriet lay unconscious, the overseer who had struck her appeared at the cabin door—not to ask about her health but to see if she was fit enough to sell. He clearly wanted to be rid of this stubborn slave girl who had dared to defy him. Several times while Harriet was recuperating, the overseer pushed open the cabin door to give prospective buyers a look at her. But, as she later recalled, "They wouldn't give a sixpence for me."

Harriet had inherited her parents' strong religious faith, and as she slowly recovered from her head

A slave auctioneer takes bids for a black woman and her daughter. Slaves were considered easier to manage once they were separated from their relatives and friends.

wound, she prayed hard—for the soul of plantation owner Edward Brodas. Years later, she told her first biographer, Sarah Bradford, about these days. "As I lay so sick on my bed, from Christmas till March, I was always praying for old master," she said. "Oh, dear Lord," she begged, "change that man's heart and make him a Christian." Although Brodas kept sending possible purchasers to look at her, she kept praying for him. "All I could say," she recalled, "was, 'Oh, Lord, convert old master.' "

Then more grim news swept the slave quarters: Brodas had decided to sell Harriet and two of her brothers and send them south in chains. At this point, Harriet recalled later, "I changed my prayer, and I said, 'Lord, if you're never going to change that man's heart, *kill him*, Lord, and take him out of the way, so he won't do more mischief.' "

Not long afterward, Brodas suddenly fell ill and died. Harriet, who never questioned the power of prayer, was horrified. What had she done? "I would [have given] the world full of silver and gold, if I had it," she said years later, "to bring that poor soul back, I would give *myself*; I would give everything! But he was gone."

Brodas's death left Harriet with a sense of deep guilt, but it also slightly improved her prospects. In his will, the plantation owner had left his estate to a young relative, directing that it be managed by Anthony Thompson, a local clergyman, until the heir came of age. Brodas's will also stipulated that none of his slaves be sold outside the state of Maryland after his death.

Thompson, however, continued Brodas's practice of hiring out the plantation's slaves. By this time, Harriet's head wound had healed, and although she suffered from violent headaches and sudden blackouts, she was once again able to work. Harriet was hired out to John Stewart, a local builder. At the same time, the estate manager rented Harriet's father, Ben Ross, to Stewart as a woodcutter. Her father, Harriet recalled later, was pleased by the assignment; he knew and respected Stewart, at least as much as any slave could respect a white southerner in those times.

At first, Harriet was assigned to work as a maid in the Stewart home. She hated every minute of it, much preferring heavy outdoor labor. At the end of three months, she begged Stewart to let her work outdoors along with the men. Aware of her unusual strength, he agreed to let her try.

Stewart soon realized Harriet Ross was worth much more as a field hand than as a domestic. She could plow, chop wood, and drive a team of oxen more efficiently than most men. Ben Ross had been put in charge of a gang of rented slaves who cut timber for the Baltimore shipyards. Harriet began working with the timber crew, swinging an ax alongside her father.

Stewart was so impressed with Harriet's energy and will to work that he allowed her a privilege given only to the most trusted slaves: When times were slack on his farm, he let her hire herself out. In return, she paid him about $50 per year; any money she earned above that was hers to keep. For the next five years, she cut timber for Stewart and, in her spare time, chopped and hauled wood for the neighbors. Gradually, she accumulated a small amount of money of her own.

Harriet Ross liked her strenuous outdoor work, and she liked the feeling of money in her pocket, no matter how little. Still, she lacked what she considered the most important thing in life. It was something mentioned only in whispers by the slaves of the South, but it was talked about more and more openly in the free states only 90 miles to the north. It was freedom.

Slave women wash their master's linens. Despising domestic work, Tubman much preferred outdoor labor—chopping trees or loading wagons along with her father and other male slaves of the Brodas plantation.

3

"A GLORY
OVER EVERYTHING"

I N THE MID-1840s, as millions of blacks toiled for their southern masters, a small but growing band of northerners worked toward ending more than two centuries of North American slavery.

The American colonies' first African slaves, a cargo of about 20 blacks, arrived at Jamestown, Virginia, in 1619. The number of slaves increased steadily; by 1763, the colonial population included about 230,000 blacks, most of them slaves. Of these, some 16,000 lived in New England, 29,000 in the Middle Colonies (New York, New Jersey, and Pennsylvania), and the remainder in the South.

Great Britain outlawed the slave trade in 1807, the United States a year later. But these moves only barred the importation of slaves; those already enslaved remained in bondage, as would their descendants. The British Empire, which included Canada, finally abolished slavery altogether in 1838. In the southern United States, however, the institution continued to flourish. Its strength rested largely on cotton.

In the late 18th century, the textile industry entered a period of rapid development in England and the northern United States. Its rise created a tre-

An Atlanta, Georgia, merchant advertises his wares: china, glass, and Negroes. Slave trading was big business in the prewar South; between 1850 and 1860 the average price of a slave increased by 70 percent.

Using inventor Eli Whitney's cotton gin, slaves rapidly remove the seeds from freshly picked cotton. Introduction of the machine vastly increased the South's cotton output; in 1860, the area produced 5 million bales.

mendous demand for southern cotton. But before it could be shipped to a textile mill, cotton had to be freed of its many sticky seeds. Seeding was a slow, labor-intensive process; even a skilled slave could clean only a few pounds of cotton per day. Then, in 1793, a Massachusetts-born inventor, Eli Whitney, developed a revolutionary new machine, the cotton engine. One slave using this engine, or "gin," as it came to be known, could clean as much cotton as four or five slaves working by hand.

Now the cultivation of cotton became hugely profitable; 10 years after Whitney invented his gin, southern cotton production had increased by 800 percent. Cotton became "king" not only in the Carolinas and Georgia but in the newly opened western lands of Alabama, Mississippi, and Louisiana. Needing more and more field hands, plantation owners turned to the long-established slave states of Virginia and Maryland. There, Edward Brodas and other slave owners began to breed and sell slaves as though they were livestock. The outlawed international slave trade was now replaced by an internal trade; thousands of blacks from the Upper South were sent to the Deep South to labor and die on the cotton plantations.

In 1860, 1 American family in 4 owned slaves; of a national population of almost 12 million, about 4 million were slaves, the vast majority of them in the South. Although a few voices were raised against slavery in the 18th century, most Americans seem to have taken the institution for granted. By the early 19th century, however, an increasing number of thoughtful people had come to see human bondage as a monstrous evil and its abolition as absolutely necessary.

In the South, slaves themselves were beginning to fight back, and in the North, free blacks took up the abolitionist cause with militant passion. Blacks and their white supporters had been deeply impressed by the actions of Toussaint L'Ouverture, a former slave who led a 1791 revolution in Haiti (then called St. Domingue). After freeing Haiti's black slaves, L'Ouverture had forced the departure of the British and the Spanish and then established the Western Hemisphere's first black republic. Another galvanic abolitionist was David Walker, a free black Bostonian. In 1829, he published *Appeal*, a fiery pamphlet that urged the slaves of the South to rise up and fight. Some historians credit Walker's powerful arguments with inspiring Nat Turner's revolt of 1831.

At the forefront of the abolitionist movement was William Lloyd Garrison, a white Massachusetts journalist and reformer. Garrison, who began publishing a journal called *The Liberator* in 1831, spoke a language that both blacks and whites could understand. "He that is with the slaveholder is against the slave," asserted Garrison. "He that is with the slave is against the slaveholder."

Most abolitionists favored gradual emancipation and payments to slave owners for their property, but Garrison demanded immediate abolition with no compensation. In the first issue of *The Liberator*, he announced that he would never compromise on slavery. "I am in earnest—I will not equivocate—I will not excuse—I will not retreat a single inch—AND I WILL BE HEARD," he thundered.

Frederick Douglass, another towering figure in the antislavery movement, was born a Maryland slave in about 1817. Escaping to Massachusetts in 1838, he became an agent of the Massachusetts Anti-Slavery Society and a tireless lecturer on abolition. In 1847, Douglass founded an abolitionist newspaper, the *North Star*, later retitled *Frederick Douglass's Paper*. As dedicated as Garrison but less radical, Douglass recruited thousands of conservative Americans to the abolitionist cause.

By 1840, about 200,000 Americans belonged to some 2,000 antislavery organizations. As their movement gained strength in the North, these people

Former slave Toussaint L'Ouverture headed a revolt in 1791 that drove British and French forces from the Caribbean island of St. Domingue. Thirteen years later, the island became Haiti, the New World's first black republic.

Publisher of the antislavery newspaper The Liberator, *William Lloyd Garrison was cofounder of the American Anti-Slavery Society and served as its president from 1843 to 1865. An uncompromising abolitionist, he urged the northern states to separate from the slaveholding South.*

began to look for practical ways to achieve their goal. Many otherwise law-abiding citizens proved willing to break the law in order to help runaway slaves escape. In the South, free blacks and other slaves were almost always willing to aid fugitive blacks. Thus was the Underground Railroad born.

According to one legend, this system of transport got its name during the 1831 pursuit of Tice Davids, a runaway Kentucky slave. When Davids reached the Ohio River, he plunged in and began a desperate swim for Ohio and freedom. His master followed closely in a boat, but when he reached the shore, his quarry had disappeared. Searching in vain, the frustrated slave owner reportedly cried, "He must have gone on an underground road!"

The Underground Railroad, of course, did not involve actual trains or tracks; it was a loose network of people willing to hide runaway slaves in their homes and "conduct" them to the next "station," or safe house. Slaves had always run away, but by the 1830s, they had allies willing to help them get out of the South and stay free. Word of these Good Samaritans began to spread through the slave quarters of the Upper South.

In 1839, news of a daring act at sea struck hope into the heart of all those who opposed slavery, black and white alike. A Spanish slave ship, the *Amistad*, was hijacked at sea by its captives, led by an African named Joseph Cinque. After killing most of the Spanish crew, the rebels sailed the ship to the coast of Long Island. There, they were arrested and jailed on charges of piracy and murder. Abolitionists across the country took up the cause of the mutineers, who eventually won their freedom in court and returned to Africa.

The *Amistad* case created a great furor. Harriet Ross and the other slaves at the Brodas plantation probably heard of it. Certainly, they were dreaming more and more of freedom.

Years afterward, Harriet Tubman told an interviewer about a recurring dream she had in those days: "I seemed to see a line, and on the other side of the line were green fields, and lovely flowers, and beautiful white ladies who stretched out their arms to me over the line, but I couldn't reach them. I always fell before I got to the line."

Such a line indeed existed. In 1767, a pair of English surveyors, Charles Mason and Jeremiah Dixon, had laid out the boundary between Pennsylvania and Maryland. That demarcation, later extended westward to mark the Pennsylvania-Virginia boundary as well, came to be known as the Mason-Dixon line. By the 1820s, the term was used to indicate the entire border between the free states of the North and the slave states of the South. Harriet Ross must have known that the line where freedom began was less than 100 miles from her home on the Eastern Shore.

In 1844, John Tubman, a free black man who lived in a cabin near the Brodas plantation, asked 24-year-old Harriet Ross to marry him. Already old for marriage by local standards, she agreed. Because his slave parents had been freed at their master's death, John Tubman had been born free. Marriage to a free man, however, did not change Harriet Tubman's slave status; it only meant that she was free to share her husband's cabin at night. Her children, if she had any, would belong to the Brodas estate.

Ironically, Harriet Tubman's husband used the slave system to control his own wife. She later said that he refused to listen to her talk about freedom and that he once told her he would betray her if she ever tried to run away. Nevertheless, she seems to have loved him; at any rate, she remained by his side for the next five years. But she never forgot her dream of freedom.

It was while she was married that Harriet Tubman learned she was being held in slavery illegally. Her

One of the nation's leading abolitionists, Frederick Douglass escaped from slavery in 1838 and published a best-selling account of his life 18 years later. A wartime adviser to President Abraham Lincoln, Douglass also served as a District of Columbia official and ambassador to Haiti.

mother, Old Rit, had often said she had been promised freedom years earlier but had been cheated out of it. Over the years, Harriet Tubman had managed to save five dollars, and in 1845, she took it to a local lawyer and asked him to look into her mother's records.

The lawyer discovered that Old Rit's original owner had willed her to one of his young relatives, specifying that the slave be freed when she reached the age of 45. But the relative had died soon afterward, and Rit had been sold despite the will's provisions. The lawyer told Tubman that her mother—and therefore she herself—was legally free. However, he said, because so much time had passed and because the women had always lived as slaves, no judge would even consider their case. With regard to black people, it seemed that justice was truly blind.

Harriet Tubman continued to suffer from blackouts, during which she often had strange and frightening dreams. She described them later as scenes from the "middle passage," the Atlantic crossing that cost the life of millions of captured Africans en route to America. She said she dreamed of ships where blacks

Slave-ship crew members in Africa, preparing for a voyage across the Atlantic Ocean, stow their human cargo below deck. Raised on firsthand reports of the dreaded "middle passage," Tubman had frequent nightmares about such journeys.

and whites fought on decks stained red with blood. She dreamed of a mother clutching a baby to her breast and leaping to her death in the sea.

Even after her marriage, Tubman lived in terror of being "sold South." During those years, she said later, "I never closed my eyes that I did not imagine that I saw the horsemen coming and heard the screams of women and children as they were being dragged away to a far worse slavery than they were enduring there." These dreams were not without foundation. Harsh as it was in the Upper South, slavery was much worse in the cotton states of Georgia, Mississippi, Alabama, and Louisiana.

In 1849, Tubman's worst fears came true. The young heir to the Brodas estate died, and word spread that his guardian planned to settle the plantation's bills by selling some of its slaves. One afternoon, Tubman learned that two of her sisters had just been sold and were already in chains, heading south. She knew it was time to go, and she persuaded three of her brothers to go with her. She told them what she had heard of the Underground Railroad and of the people in the North who would help them. Her father had showed her the North Star at night and told her how to use it as a compass; she assured her brothers she could guide them by watching it.

Tubman was reluctant to leave her husband, but she knew better than to ask him to come along—or even let him know she was going. He had already promised to betray her. She left late at night with her brothers, but they soon began to drag their feet. Even though she urged them on, they went slower and slower, worrying about what would happen when they were missed. Signs would be posted everywhere; alarm bells would be rung; the dogs would be set loose; and mounted patrollers with whips would track them down. They had no food, no money, no friends, and they were heading for unfamiliar country. Slavery,

Kidnapped by Spanish slavers in 1839, Joseph Cinque led his fellow prisoners in a revolt at sea. After killing most of their captors, the Africans sailed the slave ship to New York, where they were jailed, tried, and eventually freed.

A column of southbound slaves, chained to each other at wrist and ankle, makes its way through Washington, D.C. Tubman and her fellow slaves lived in constant fear of being "sold south"—led in chains to the Deep South's plantations, where living and working conditions were unbearable.

bad as it was, was at least familiar. The brothers feared the unknown. They turned back and made their sister turn back with them.

She crept back into her sleeping husband's bed, bitterly disappointed. But she had learned an important lesson, one she would never forget: Freedom is only for those bold enough to take it.

Two days after the botched escape, a slave from a nearby plantation gave Tubman bad news: She had been sold and was scheduled to start south the next day. This time she knew she would have to run alone. Years later, she described her thoughts at that moment: "There was one of two things I had a *right* to, liberty or death; if I could not have one, I would have the other; for no man should take me alive; I should fight for my liberty as long as my strength lasted, and when the time came for me to go, the Lord would let them take me."

Tubman wanted someone in her family to know she was leaving on her own, that she was not on her way south. After her last experience, she would not tell her brothers. How could she relay the news safely? Legend has it that she made her way toward "the big house," where one of her sisters was working in the kitchen. Walking back and forth near the window, Tubman sang an old spiritual:

> I'll meet you in the morning,
> When I reach the Promised Land,
> On the other side of Jordan.
> For I'm bound for the Promised Land.

That night, after her husband was asleep, Harriet Tubman wrapped up a little cornbread and salt herring, then tucked her favorite patchwork quilt under her arm. Did she kiss John Tubman good-bye as he slept? Did she regret leaving him? No one will ever know, for she never said. But perhaps she hinted at her feelings in her choice of a name: For the rest of her life, she identified herself as "Mrs. Tubman."

Tubman had heard of a local white woman who was said to help runaways, and she made her way through the woods to the woman's house. When she saw Tubman at her door, the woman seemed to know what her visitor wanted. She invited her in, then gave her two slips of paper, explaining that each contained the name of a family on the road north. When Tubman presented the slips, said the woman, these people would give her food and tell her how to get to the next house. The slips of paper were Tubman's first "tickets" on the Underground Railroad. In gratitude, Tubman gave the woman her precious quilt, then started on her way.

Reaching the first house just after dawn, Tubman presented her slip of paper. The woman of the house responded by giving her a broom and telling her to sweep the walk. Tubman was shocked. Was this a betrayal? Was she now this woman's slave? But she soon realized the move was for camouflage. A black woman with a broom would hardly be noticed, certainly not suspected as a runaway.

As soon as night fell, the woman's husband put Tubman in the back of his farm wagon, covered her with vegetables, and drove her north to the next "station." In this way, sometimes helped by others, sometimes left to her own devices, Harriet Tubman made her way north, walking up the Eastern Shore peninsula toward Pennsylvania. She began to learn the route she was to use so often and so effectively in the future.

Traveling by night, hiding in the daylight, Tubman trudged through 90 miles of swamp and woodland. At last, many days after she started, she found herself across the magic line, on free soil. Years later, she said of that morning: "I looked at my hands to see if I was the same person now that I was free. There was such a glory over everything; the sun came like gold through the trees, and over the fields, and I felt like I was in heaven." ❧

4

"A FRIEND
WITH FRIENDS"

———— ⟨⟩ ————

I WAS FREE but there was no one to welcome me to freedom," recalled Harriet Tubman. "I was a stranger in a strange land."

Years later, Tubman talked to biographer Sarah Bradford about her arrival in Pennsylvania in 1849. "To this solemn resolution I came," she said. "I was free, and [my parents, brothers, and sisters] should be free also; I would make a home for them in the North, and the Lord helping me, I would bring them all there. Oh, how I prayed then, lying all alone on the cold, damp ground. 'Oh, dear Lord,' I said, 'I ain't got no friend but you. Come to my help, Lord, for I'm in trouble!' "

Tubman, however, was no woman to wait for help to come to her. Making her way to Philadelphia, she managed to get a job in a hotel kitchen. She spent the winter cooking, washing dishes, saving her money, and thinking about how she could rescue her family from Maryland. At that time, Philadelphia was second only to Boston as a center of abolitionist sentiment; the city was home not only to many whites working toward emancipation but also to a large number of blacks, some of them legally free, some of them escaped slaves like Tubman.

Horse-drawn traffic rumbles through the cobbled streets of mid-19th-century Philadelphia. Tubman, who arrived in the bustling Pennsylvania city in 1849, wasted no time in finding herself a job; she signed on as a hotel cook and dishwasher.

The Philadelphia Vigilance Committee greets Henry ''Box'' Brown, a slave who escaped from Virginia in a wooden crate. Clergyman James Miller McKim stands at the far left; next to him is William Still, who kept a written record of the fugitive slaves who passed through Philadelphia.

Both blacks and whites in Philadelphia (and the rest of the North) had been galvanized by the passage of the Fugitive Slave Act of 1850. Under this federal legislation, any Negro accused of being a runaway could be brought before a federal judge or a special commissioner. Denied a jury trial or even the right to testify on his or her own behalf, the alleged runaway could easily be returned to slavery. All the law required was a sworn statement from a white individual who claimed to be the black person's owner. The law also provided heavy penalties for anyone who helped a slave escape. Many northerners, even some who were not abolitionists, believed that the Fugitive Slave Act violated both the Constitution and basic human rights.

Soon after Congress passed the infamous law, Harriet Tubman paid a call on the Philadelphia Vigilance Committee. This organization, formed to assist fugitive slaves, was managed by two of the Underground Railroad's busiest "station masters": white clergyman James Miller McKim and William Still, a freeborn black Pennsylvanian. Still managed to meet just about every escaping slave who passed through Philadelphia. He fed them, listened to their stories, and helped them plan the next stage of their journey, no matter what the danger to himself.

One celebrated incident in McKim and Still's career involved Henry Brown, a slave from Richmond, Virginia. Brown persuaded a sympathetic white friend to nail him into a wooden packing box and ship it to the Vigilance Committee's office. After 25 hours in the small, suffocating crate, a beaming Brown emerged to greet the astonished Still and McKim. For the rest of his life, the ingenious escapee was known as "Box" Brown.

Unlike most of the fugitive slaves he helped, Still could read and write, and he used his talents well. He interviewed the runaways who passed through and recorded their names and stories in a ledger. It was Still's hope that one day all slaves would be free, and that when that day came, families might be able to trace their relatives through his records. He kept his ledger hidden in a graveyard, but in 1872, when it was at last safe to make it public, he published it under the title *The Underground Rail Road.* Still's book, one of the few written records of the legendary slave-escape system, has proved a gold mine to students of American history.

Tubman took to making frequent visits to Still's office, where she met and talked with many fugitive slaves. Meanwhile, she saved her pennies to help finance the trip she planned, back to the Eastern Shore to bring her family across the Mason-Dixon line. As it turned out, her first trip as a conductor was not to the Eastern Shore but to Baltimore, across the Chesapeake Bay.

Author Ann Petry described Tubman's first return to the South in her 1955 book, *Harriet Tubman: Conductor on the Underground Railway.* One night, according to Petry, Tubman was paying a call on Still and McKim when a stranger appeared, asking for help. He wanted the Vigilance Committee's assistance in rescuing a black woman and her two children from Cambridge, Maryland. The woman's husband was a free man, said the visitor, but his wife and children were about to be auctioned off to slave traders from the Deep South.

The visiting abolitionist said a local Quaker (a member of the Religious Society of Friends, a pacifist Christian sect) might be able to get the family out of Cambridge; but they would need someone to pilot them across the dangerous stretch from Baltimore to Philadelphia. As he outlined the escape plan, he mentioned the name of the free husband: John Bowley. Tubman must have looked startled; Bowley was her brother-in-law, husband of her sister Mary.

Baltimore, shown here in an 1849 photograph, was known as a dangerous spot for fugitives. The Philadelphia Vigilance Committee's William Still tried to talk Tubman out of going to the Maryland city in 1850, but she knew she was needed there, and she went.

At once, Tubman announced that she herself would go to Baltimore and guide the Bowley family to safety. Still objected. Tubman, he noted, was still a fugitive herself, and Baltimore was a dangerous city for runaways. Travel, too, was extremely hazardous. Blacks who tried to board trains, even in the company of their masters, were weighed and measured like sacks of grain so they could be compared with the ever-growing list of runaways.

But Tubman insisted. She knew the land, she said; she had crossed it herself. And she could leave at once. Time was growing short, and the mission would have to be accomplished quickly. Reluctantly, Still agreed to let Tubman try.

On the day of the Cambridge auction, a black man claiming to belong to the auctioneer came to the slave pen during the noontime break. He gave the guard an official-looking letter, requesting him to turn the female captive and her children over to the bearer; the slaves, said the letter, were to be taken to the hotel where the auctioneer was having lunch.

The "auctioneer's slave" was John Bowley, and his official letter had been forged by his Quaker ally. Sensing nothing amiss, the guard unlocked the pen. Bowley marched his family through the streets of Cambridge to the home of his Quaker accomplice. The Quaker hid the fugitives in his attic until nightfall, then escorted them to the river. There, a small sailboat awaited them.

An experienced seaman, Bowley hustled his family aboard and set sail for the North. When he spotted the prearranged signal, one blue and one yellow lantern, he brought the boat ashore. A white woman met the fugitives, concealed them in a wagonload of potatoes, and took them to a brick house.

Bowley knocked on the door, and a voice from inside said, "Who's there?" He responded with the password: "A friend with friends." The door flew open, and Harriet Tubman rushed out to embrace her relatives. With her precious "shipment" in tow, Tubman made it back to Philadelphia safely, as indeed she was always to make it. "I never ran my train off the track," she proudly noted years later, "and I never lost a passenger."

Baltimore, as Still had pointed out, was a dangerous place for a fugitive slave, but the Eastern Shore was even more perilous. Nevertheless, it was there that Tubman's remaining family lived, and it was there she went. She made her first trip to Dorchester County in the spring of 1851. When she returned to Philadelphia, she brought one of her brothers and two other men, whom she entrusted to Still's care. She worked all that summer and fall, saving money for a trip she had dreamed of ever since the day she first left Maryland.

A slave pen, built to hold blacks designated for auction, stands ready to receive its human merchandise. It was from such an enclosure that Tubman's brother-in-law, John Bowley, spirited his wife and children out of Cambridge, Maryland, and into Tubman's arms.

Fugitive slave Thomas Sims (second row, center), after his 1851 arrest by Boston marshal Charles Devins, is escorted to the ship that will return him to Georgia. Boston's Vigilance Committee plastered the city with copies of a poster (opposite) warning all blacks to be wary of slave catchers after Sims was captured. (Despite a major attempt to rescue him, Sims was returned to Georgia. In 1863, he escaped again. In 1877, he showed up in Washington, D.C., where he was employed by the U.S. attorney general—Charles Devins, the man who had sent him back to slavery 26 years earlier.)

In December, Tubman made her way back down the peninsula to Dorchester County. She had to exercise extraordinary caution, because this was an area where she was well known. When she arrived at the Brodas plantation just after dark one evening, she went directly to her husband's cabin. Perhaps she hesitated before approaching his door. He had, after all, often ridiculed her dreams of freedom and had even threatened to betray her. What kind of welcome would she get? She knocked on the door. It swung open to reveal John Tubman—and a young, attractive black woman.

When Harriet Tubman told her husband she had come back for him, he laughed in her face. The young woman at his side, he said, was now his wife, and he had no interest in going anywhere. Late that night, Harriet Tubman left the plantation with several slaves and never looked back. She never laid eyes on John Tubman again and rarely spoke of him.

That was Tubman's third trip to the South. By now, she had developed the routes and techniques that would serve her so well as she conducted her people to freedom. Although every step was risky, Tubman's familiarity with the roads, the hiding places, and the "depots" allowed her to travel with increasing assurance.

On her rescue expeditions, Tubman usually traveled in Delaware as far as possible before crossing into Maryland. Delaware offered several advantages. First, it contained the headwaters of most of the rivers that drained the Eastern Shore, which meant she could use a small boat to reach almost any point. Even more important, Delaware was home to many more free black men and women than slaves. The state's black population in 1860 was 21,627, of whom only 1,798 were slaves. Delaware was, in fact, the only state in the South where a black person was assumed to be free unless proven to be a slave. Tubman could thus cross the state fairly openly, at least on the way down.

Tubman's return route took her past a number of Underground Railroad stations, or safe houses. When she approached one, she would hide her "passengers," then knock at the door. When someone responded from inside, she would answer with the magic words: "A friend with friends."

On most of Tubman's trips from the South, her last stop was Wilmington, Delaware, a city right on the Mason-Dixon line. Wilmington was the home of Quaker Thomas Garrett, a remarkable man who would become one of Tubman's closest friends. Garrett owned a large shoe store; when fleeing slaves arrived at his door, he hid them behind a false wall in his shop. He also provided each runaway with a pair of shoes, for many the first they had ever owned. According to William Still's records, Garrett helped some 2,700 slaves escape.

CAUTION!!
COLORED PEOPLE
OF BOSTON, ONE & ALL,
You are hereby respectfully CAUTIONED and advised, to avoid conversing with the
Watchmen and Police Officers of Boston,
For since the recent ORDER OF THE MAYOR & ALDERMEN, they are empowered to act as
KIDNAPPERS
AND
Slave Catchers,
And they have already been actually employed in KIDNAPPING, CATCHING, AND KEEPING SLAVES. Therefore, if you value your LIBERTY, and the Welfare of the Fugitives among you, Shun them in every possible manner, as so many HOUNDS on the track of the most unfortunate of your race.
Keep a Sharp Look Out for KIDNAPPERS, and have TOP EYE open.
APRIL 24, 1851.
THEODORE PARKER'S PLACARD

Several times arrested, found guilty, and heavily fined for assisting runaways, Garrett finally lost both his shoe business and his sizable personal fortune. Undeterred, he went back to work at the age of 60 and continued to help fugitives. He was arrested and fined again; this time, the presiding judge said he hoped the experience would teach Garrett to stop interfering "with the cause of justice by helping off runaway Negroes." Garrett, who spoke in the Quakers' biblical phrases, rose, looked hard at the judge, and said, "Friend, thee hasn't left me a dollar, but I wish to say to thee . . . that if anyone knows of a fugitive who wants a shelter, and a friend, *send him to Thomas Garrett!*"

In an 1868 letter to Sarah Bradford, Garrett referred with awe to "the remarkable labors" of Tubman. "In truth, I never met with any person, of any color, who had more confidence in the voice of God, as spoken direct to her soul," he said. "She has declared to me that she felt no more fear of being arrested by her former master . . . when in his immediate neighborhood, than she did in the State of New York, or Canada, for she said she ventured only where God sent her."

A runaway black family arrives at an Underground Railroad station. Operated by a loosely organized network of abolitionists, the Railroad consisted of a series of way stations where fugitives could rest, eat, and get directions to the next stop. Some historians believe that as many as 75,000 blacks escaped to freedom via the U.G.R.R., as the system was sometimes called.

By 1851, the Fugitive Slave Act was taking a heavy toll of runaways. Tubman heard ominous news of fugitive slaves arrested and returned to the South from such previously safe cities as Boston and Syracuse, New York. Abolitionists were outraged. "The only way to make the Fugitive Slave Act a dead letter," said former slave Frederick Douglass, "is to make a half dozen or more dead kidnappers."

Free blacks and their allies in the North began to fight back. In Boston, 300 armed men were needed to send 1 fugitive back to the South. The Fugitive Slave Act backfired in the long run because it increased northern opposition to slavery; yet it succeeded in making life difficult for Harriet Tubman. No longer able to work safely in Philadelphia, she moved to St. Catharines, Canada, a small town near Niagara Falls where many free blacks and former slaves had settled.

Between 1851 and 1857, Tubman made two trips to the Eastern Shore each year, one in the fall and one in the spring. Now instead of 90 miles, she had to conduct her passengers on a grueling journey of almost 500 miles. But the trips brought her people to genuine freedom, and they gave her the chance to meet the leaders of the abolitionist movement, many of whom lived in New York State and New England. It was on these pilgrimages that she met and befriended such giants of the movement as Frederick Douglass, Gerrit Smith, J. W. Loguen, and John Brown, the man who would most inspire her.

John Brown (seen here in an early portrait) was to leave an indelible imprint on American history—and on Tubman. Along with the rest of the nation, Tubman probably first heard of the fiery abolitionist in 1856, when he staged a series of spectacular raids on proslavery settlements in Kansas Territory.

5

"MOVE OR DIE!"

❦

ALREADY, PEOPLE WERE calling her Moses. She traveled light and she traveled fast.

She knew the places where it was safe to hide: drainage ditches, hedges, and abandoned sheds or tobacco barns. Sometimes, she concealed her fugitives in potato holes, board-lined pits where farmers stored their winter vegetables. Once, she and her group hid in a manure pile and breathed through straws.

In addition to such hideouts, there were the more comfortable way stations, most of them operated by Quakers or free black people. Residents of the Cooper House in Camden, New Jersey, for example, regularly hid fugitives in a bunk-room over their kitchen. Another stopover for fleeing blacks was in Odessa, Delaware, where the Friends Meeting House (the Quaker version of a church) had a concealed loft over the sanctuary.

Harriet Tubman always carried a revolver on the Underground Railroad, and she was always ready to use it. "She could not read or write, but she had military genius," a contemporary said of her.

Tubman's standard procedure was to gather money and supplies in the North and then slip down the Eastern Shore, through Delaware and into Mary-

Tubman holds a musket in this engraving, but her choice of weapons was usually a pistol. Carrying her weapon—and willing to use it—the Underground Railroad conductor enforced iron discipline on the sometimes faint-hearted fugitives she escorted to freedom.

This clergyman's residence in Ripley, Ohio, was among the Underground Railroad's busiest stations. High on a bluff over-looking the Ohio River, the house could easily be seen by escaping Kentucky slaves on the river's opposite bank.

land. There, she would make contact with the slaves who were ready to escape. She usually led them away on Saturday night, hoping they would not be missed and pursued until Monday. Before heading out, she paid someone to take down the wanted posters that would be sure to appear across the countryside.

In a 1907 article, the New York *Herald* described Tubman's methods:

> On some darkly propitious night there would be breathed about the Negro quarters of a plantation word that she had come to lead them forth. At midnight, she would stand waiting in the depths of woodland or timbered swamp, and stealthily, one by one, her fugitives would creep to the rendezvous. She entrusted her plans to but few of the party. . . . She knew her path well by this time, and they followed her unerring guidance without question. She assumed the authority and enforced the discipline of a military despot.

Once the slaves had left, there was no turning back. Tubman knew too well what happened to runaways who returned: They were beaten until they revealed their escape plans and the names of the people who had aided them. She would allow no one to betray her routes and secrets.

More than once, a slave grew fainthearted and wanted to go back, just as her brothers had the first time she tried to run away. Sometimes they were men twice her size. But now she was prepared. The hesitant slave would feel the cold steel of a revolver at his head and hear Tubman's voice harsh in his ear: "Move or die!" They moved. None of her passengers ever turned back, and she never lost one. To keep babies from crying, Tubman sometimes drugged them with opium, then readily available. When their mothers grew tired, she carried the babies in a basket on her arm.

To raise the flagging spirits of her followers, Tubman often sang to them as they plodded through woods and swamps. Hearing her strong, husky voice, the weary fugitives often joined in. The spiritual they most often sang referred to the biblical Moses' delivery of his people from Egyptian bondage:

You may hinder me here, but you can't up there,
Let my people go.
He sits in the heavens and answers prayer,
Let my people go!

Oh go down, Moses,
Way down in Egypt land,
Tell old Pharaoh,
Let my people go.

Tubman's blackouts still came upon her at unexpected times. She would simply collapse by the side of the road, and her passengers could only watch and wait until she awakened; then they would be off again. Sometimes, Tubman would steal a slave owner's buggy for the first stage of the journey. She knew the neighbors would assume the slaves were out on an errand for their master. When the horses grew winded, Tubman would abandon the buggy and continue the trip on foot, by boat, or in a cart heaped with vegetables.

Conductor Tubman became an expert at disguise and deception. Once, when she had to enter the village where her former master lived, she disguised herself as an old slave bringing chickens to market. The New York *Herald* told the story 50 years later: "As she turned a corner she saw coming toward her none other than her old master. Lest he might see through her impersonation, and to make an excuse for flight, she loosed the cord that held the fowls and amid the laughter of the bystanders, gave chase to them as they flew squawking over a nearby fence." In her 1869 biography of Tubman, Sarah Bradford added, "And [the master] went on his way, little thinking that he was brushing the very garments of the woman who had dared to steal herself, and others of his belongings."

On another occasion, Tubman disguised herself by pretending to read a book—hoping she was holding it right side up. Soon she heard one man whisper to another: "This can't be the woman. The one we want can't read or write."

By 1854, the woman called Moses was well known throughout the Eastern Shore, a legend among the slaves and a demon to the slaveholders. Try as they might, the plantation owners never got so much as a glimpse of this mysterious figure who came to the slave cabins at night and spirited away their valuable property.

In late 1854, Tubman got word that three of her brothers, Benjamin, John, and William Henry Ross, were going to be sold south the day after Christmas. It was time for a trip to Dorchester County. Tubman had a friend write to Jacob Jackson, a literate black man who lived near the estate where her brothers worked as hired slaves. "Read my letter to the old folks [Old Ben and Rit], and give my love to them," said the letter. "Tell my brothers to be always watching unto prayer, and when the good old ship of Zion comes along, to be ready to step on board."

On Christmas Eve, Tubman arrived on the East-ern Shore. Collecting her brothers, 2 other men, and a young woman, she headed for her parents' cabin, some 40 miles to the north. She would not take Ben and Rit this time; she knew that at their advanced age they were unlikely to be sold and shipped south. The group left in such a hurry that Tubman's brother William Henry had to leave his wife and newborn baby, promising to return for them soon. When it was time to go, Tubman waited for no one.

When the party arrived at Ben and Rit's cabin, they hid in an outbuilding where feed corn was stored. The parents knew nothing of the escape plan. Tub-man longed to see her mother, but she knew the old woman was unable to keep a secret and would tell the whole neighborhood. To make matters worse, Rit had been expecting her sons all day and had killed and cooked a pig for them. Tubman sent the two extra men to the cabin; they called Old Ben out into

Fugitives arrive at the Ohio farm of Levi Coffin, a dedicated sup-porter of the Underground Rail-road. Like his fellow Quaker Thomas Garrett of Wilmington, Coffin made no secret of the hos-pitality, financial assistance, and transportation he provided to fleeing slaves.

Louisiana runaways rest before heading north. Faced with immense distances through hostile country, fugitives from the cotton states were far more likely to be killed or captured than were those escaping from the Upper South.

the night and told him what was going on. He promised to keep the secret from Rit and said he would bring the hungry travelers some food.

Ben Ross, a slave for almost 50 years, had earned a widespread reputation for honesty. Indeed, he must have doubted his own ability to lie, for when he visited his children in the corncrib, he averted his eyes and never looked directly at them. And later, on Christmas Day, when he said good-bye to them, he tied a bandanna over his eyes.

Tubman and her passengers headed north toward freedom. A few days later, a team of slave chasers brought a report to the man who owned Ben and Rit. The men said they had questioned the fugitives' parents. They found the old woman heartbroken because she had been expecting her boys for Christmas. And the old man said he had not laid eyes on his children. The slaveholder accepted the story. He knew Ben Ross was no liar.

"Moses arrives with six passengers," noted the Vigilance Committee's William Still when Tubman brought her fugitives into Philadelphia. "Great fears were entertained for her safety, but she seemed wholly devoid of personal fear," wrote Still in his ledger. "The idea of being captured by slave-hunters or slaveholders, seemed never to enter her mind." Still added that he found it "obvious" that Tubman's "success in going into Maryland as she did was attributable to her adventurous spirit and utter disregard of consequences. Her like it is probable was never known before or since."

After escorting her brothers and their friends to Canada, Tubman prepared for her next mission. This one, undertaken in November 1856, involved a woman and three men. One of the men, Josiah Bailey, was the kind of slave every master wanted. Strong, healthy, and skilled as a farmer, he never talked back or gave any trouble. Bailey had been rented out by his master for six years to a planter named William Hughlett. In 1856, Hughlett decided to buy Bailey. He paid $2,000, a steep price but worth it to the purchaser, who planned to save money by making Bailey his overseer.

The day he bought him, Hughlett gave Bailey a savage whipping. The slave had done no wrong, said the master, but he needed to learn who owned him. Bailey submitted silently but, he later told Tubman, he said to himself, "This is the first and the last." That night he "borrowed" a rowboat and made his painful way down the river to Rit and Ben Ross's cabin. Speaking to Ross alone, he said, "The next time Moses comes, let me know."

Tubman arrived soon afterward. With Bailey and the other escapees, she headed north, closely followed by a small army of slave catchers. Because Bailey was so valuable, his master offered an unusually high reward for his capture. Hughlett posted signs all through the Eastern Shore. They showed the South's symbol of a runaway, a black figure with a knapsack and a walking stick. The signs read:

Heavy Reward
Two Thousand Six Hundred Dollars

After describing the runaways, the signs—which Bailey read to Tubman and the others—said that $1,500 was for Josiah Bailey alone; the rest was for the other slaves. Separate posters announced an even higher reward for a certain black woman. Harriet Tubman, "sometimes called Moses," was worth $12,000 to any person who delivered her to the authorities. The countryside swarmed with bounty hunters, but Tubman knew the Eastern Shore better than any of her pursuers. At one point, she led her shivering people across a deep creek, using a hidden ford that she said she had seen in a dream.

For the first time Tubman had a helper. Tough and courageous, Josiah Bailey pushed the group forward, singing in a low voice. Among his favorite verses was this one:

Who comes yonder all dressed in red?
I heard the angels singing—
It's all the children Moses led,
I heard the angels singing.

Keeping to the fields and hedges, the party made it as far as Wilmington, but they found the Delaware River bridge heavily guarded. Wanted posters were everywhere. Tubman scattered her group, placing them in the homes of sympathetic free blacks. She believed her friend Thomas Garrett would find a way to help, and she was right. Garrett sent a wagonload of bricklayers across the bridge; when they returned to Wilmington that night, seemingly drunk, they carried five black fugitives hidden under the bricks.

From Wilmington, Tubman led the group to Philadelphia, then on to New York City. The trip had gone as well it could have, but Bailey was growing discouraged. He had thought they would be safe in the North, but the wanted posters were on every wall here, too. When the fugitives walked into the office of the New York Anti-Slavery Society, its president, Oliver Johnson, shook Bailey's hand and said jokingly, "Well, Joe, I'm glad to see the man whose head is worth $1,500!"

Bailey did not laugh. "How did you know me?" he asked. Johnson showed him a copy of the poster and said that anyone who read it would recognize Bailey easily. That meant that anywhere between New York and Canada—a distance of more than 300 miles—someone might pounce on him and drag him off for the reward. Disheartened, Bailey begged Tubman and the others to go on to Canada without him. With him along, he said, they were all bound to be caught. Tubman, of course, refused.

The rest of the trip north was easier. Much of the Underground Railroad's route through New York State involved real trains; Tubman and her charges traveled in a baggage car, watched over by a sympathetic trainman. But Bailey, Tubman later told Sarah Bradford, "was silent. He talked no more. He sang no more. He sat with his head on his hand, and nobody could rouse him, or make him take any interest in anything."

When the train approached Niagara Falls, the conductor took the group into a coach so they could see Canada on the other side of the bridge. Even there, they were still in danger. Until the train

The figure of a fleeing black often appeared on the South's wanted posters, most of which offered rewards. Few escapees, however, were worth as much to bounty hunters as Tubman; the price on her head was $12,000.

Nineteenth-century painter Thomas Mason caught the sense of terror felt by blacks who braved storms, swamps, and snarling dogs in their quest for freedom. Tubman must also have known fear on her many rescue missions, but by all accounts, she never showed it.

reached the center of the bridge, any slave catcher could legally arrest them and drag them all back into slavery. But the train moved steadily across the great iron bridge. When it reached the center, Tubman gave Bailey a shake and shouted, "Joe, you're in Queen Victoria's dominions! You're a free man!"

Bailey used his voice for the first time in days. With tears streaming down his face, he looked up and began to sing, "Glory to God and Jesus too, One more soul is safe!" He kept on singing, even after the train had stopped on the Canadian shore. A crowd of curious white people gathered around him on the platform, staring as he bellowed, "There's only one more journey for me now, and that's to heaven."

Tubman tugged at his sleeve, trying to quiet him. "Well, you old fool," she joked. "You might have looked at the Falls first and gone to heaven afterwards!" ◆

6

"THE GREATEST
HEROINE OF
THE AGE"

THE 1850s BEGAN with the passage of the infamous Fugitive Slave Act and ended with violence and bloodshed at Harpers Ferry, Virginia. In the years between, the storm clouds that had been gathering in the 1830s and 1840s grew darker. North and South eyed each other with increasing mistrust. The United States moved steadily toward division.

The abolitionist movement had been intensifying its crusade against slavery from the 1830s on. By the 1850s, a battalion of popular lecturers was sweeping through the North, driving home the message that slavery was a sin. Among the most effective speakers were such former slaves as Frederick Douglass and such white abolitionists as Wendell Phillips, an aristocratic Bostonian who later served as president of the Anti-Slavery Society. In Congress, Senator Charles Sumner of Massachusetts and other pro-abolition legislators made passionate speeches, which they transcribed and mailed to thousands of voters. Many northern newspapers, including the powerful New York *Tribune*, took an unreserved stand against slavery. Perhaps the most irresistible abolitionist message, however, was delivered by a remarkable book, *Uncle Tom's Cabin*.

Published by the American Anti-Slavery Society, an 1835 handbill shows an image widely used in abolitionist literature: a chained slave asking, "Am I not a man and a brother?" The Anti-Slavery Society, formed in 1833, flooded the North with such emotional appeals.

61

Abolitionist orator Wendell Phillips addresses an antislavery meeting on Boston Common. An admirer and good friend of Tubman's, Phillips served as president of the Anti-Slavery Society from 1865 to 1870.

Written by New Englander Harriet Beecher Stowe and published in 1852, *Uncle Tom's Cabin* struck America like a thunderbolt. Set in the plantation South, the novel tells the story of a devoutly Christian slave, Tom, and his friends and fellow slaves, George and Eliza Harris. George escapes from his cruel master, planning to buy his wife and son's freedom as soon as he can. Meanwhile, Eliza learns that circumstances have forced her kindhearted owner, Mr. Shelby, to sell both Tom and her son, Harry. Desperate, she flees with Harry.

Tom is shipped south, where he saves the life of Eva, a six-year-old white girl. Eva's grateful father, Augustine St. Clair, then buys Tom, but both St. Clair and his daughter soon die. Tom is bought by the sadistic Simon Legree, who viciously mistreats the patient old slave. Eliza and George Harris manage to escape with their boy to Canada, but Tom meets a grim fate. Just as George Shelby, the son of his former master, arrives to buy him back, Tom is beaten to death by Legree. Appalled, Shelby denounces slavery and becomes an abolitionist.

The first edition of *Uncle Tom's Cabin* sold out within a week of publication; little more than a year later, sales reached 1 million. The book, described by historian J. C. Furnas as "a verbal earthquake, an ink-and-paper tidal wave," sparked a wave of hatred against slavery, even among many previously neutral northerners. In the novel's wake came a flood of "Tom shows," popular dramatic portrayals of the horribly mistreated but always forgiving Uncle Tom.

According to Sarah Bradford, Tubman's friends once tried to persuade her to attend a Philadelphia performance of *Uncle Tom.* "I've heard *Uncle Tom's Cabin* read," she reportedly replied, "and I tell you, Mrs. Stowe's pen hasn't begun to paint what slavery is. . . . I've seen the *real thing,* and I don't want to see it on any stage."

The slavery issue continued to occupy the national stage as well, fanning ever-deeper anger between North and South. In 1857, the United States Supreme Court finally expressed its opinion on the issue, but instead of soothing the interregional quarrel, the Court's decision heightened it. The case involved Dred Scott, a Missouri slave whose master had taken him to the free territory of Minnesota and then back to the slave state of Missouri. Claiming that residence in free territory had made him a free man, Scott sued for freedom from his master. When the state supreme court decided against Scott, his abolitionist lawyers took his case to the U.S. Supreme Court.

After hearing lengthy arguments on both sides of the question, Chief Justice Roger B. Taney issued the Court's majority opinion. Scott, said Taney, was not a citizen and had no right to sue in a federal court. The Constitution had created a white man's government, and Negroes, "beings of an inferior order," had "no rights which a white man was bound to respect." Furthermore, stated the chief justice, Scott's resi-

Uncle Tom and Little Eva, characters in Harriet Beecher Stowe's Uncle Tom's Cabin, *appear on a 19th-century theatrical poster. "Tom shows"—stage versions of Stowe's best-selling novel about slavery—swept the nation in the 1860s, but Tubman refused to attend one. "I've seen the real thing," she said.*

dence in a free territory had not affected his status as a slave; he was property, and the Constitution forbade anyone to deprive a man of his property without "due process of law."

Meanwhile, a young Illinois politician named Abraham Lincoln was making a name for himself by engaging in public debates on the slavery issue. Like many Americans in the North and the Midwest, Lincoln—whose oratorical skills would help carry him to the White House—opposed slavery on moral, political, and ethical grounds. He did not, however, support social and political equality for blacks.

In Lincoln's view, slavery presented a threat to white Americans. If the United States accepted the idea that blacks were not created with equal rights, he said, it might next deny equal rights to other groups. "As a nation," Lincoln said in 1855, "we began by declaring that 'all men are created equal.' We now practically read it 'all men are created equal, except negroes.' " At that rate, continued the Illinois Republican, "it will [soon] read 'all men are created equal, except negroes and foreigners, and catholics.' "

Lincoln opposed the extension of slavery into the territories because, he said, white free labor would be unable to compete with black slave labor. Although his views would become less conservative over the years, in the 1850s Lincoln maintained that if slavery were confined to the South, it would eventually die of its own accord. Given enough time, he said, the "wrong" of human bondage would disappear from the United States.

As Lincoln addressed the citizens of Illinois about slavery, people were fighting and dying over the issue in the territory known as "bleeding Kansas." Soon after Kansas Territory was opened for settlement in 1854, large numbers of pioneers moved there. While most of the newcomers came to establish farms, many came to determine the status of slavery in the terri-

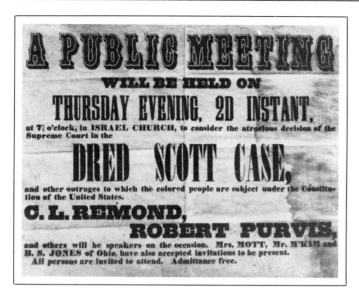

An 1857 poster advertises a meeting to protest "the atrocious decision of the Supreme Court in the Dred Scott case." The decision labeled blacks "an inferior order" and said they had "no rights which a white man was bound to respect."

tory. Both dedicated Free-Soilers and equally ardent supporters of slavery poured into Kansas, each side ready to fight for its beliefs.

In 1856, a band of proslavery adherents attacked the town of Lawrence, killing several antislavery residents. In revenge, John Brown, a fiercely dedicated white abolitionist who believed that God had appointed him to destroy slavery, attacked the proslavery settlement of Pottawatomie and killed five people. As a result of the 2 raids, civil conflict broke out in Kansas; more than 200 settlers died in the guerrilla warfare between the 2 factions.

In this climate of violence and turmoil, Harriet Tubman continued her work, traveling to the Eastern Shore, meeting with slaves who wanted to escape, and telling them about the North's abolition movement. During the mid-1850s, she began giving certain groups of runaways directions to Underground Railroad stations and sending them off on their own. In other cases, she escorted groups of escapees as far as Philadelphia or New York, left them in charge of friends there, then headed back south for more passengers. When Tubman felt unsure that a group of escaping slaves would be able to make the trip without her, she accompanied them all the way from Maryland to Canada. Tubman had now become a regular on the route that led north from New York City to Troy and Albany, then west across the Mohawk Valley to Niagara Falls and free Canada.

In 1855, journalist Benjamin Drew visited several Canadian towns where free blacks had settled. In the village of St. Catharines, Drew met and interviewed the celebrated woman known as Moses. He asked her to comment on slavery and recorded her response in his 1856 book, *The Refugee; or Narratives of Fugitive Slaves*:

> I grew up like a neglected weed—ignorant of liberty, having no experience of it. I was not happy or contented: Every time I saw a white man I was afraid of being carried away. . . . We were always uneasy. Now I've been free, I know what slavery is. . . . I think slavery is the next thing to hell. If a person would send another into bondage, he would, it appears to me, be bad enough to send him to hell if he could.

About a year after she talked to Drew, Tubman made her first visit to Boston, where she was invited to attend an antislavery meeting. Historian, playwright, and novelist William Wells Brown, a former slave who had become an ardent abolitionist and a popular speaker, noted her presence in one of his many books, *The Rising Son; or the Antecedents and Advancements of the Colored Race*:

> For eight or ten years previous to the breaking out of the Rebellion [the Civil War], all who frequented antislavery conventions, lectures, picnics, and fairs could not fail to have seen a black woman of medium size, upper front teeth gone, smiling countenance, attired in coarse, but neat apparel, with an old-fashioned reticule or bag suspended by her side, and who, on taking her seat, would at once drop off into a sound sleep.

Tubman, said Brown, became a frequent visitor at the homes of Boston's leading abolitionists. These highly educated, cultured men and women would listen spellbound as Tubman, who could neither read nor write, discussed slavery and abolition. Brown found himself awed by Tubman. "Men from Canada, who had made their escape years before, and whose families were still in the prison-house of slavery, would seek out Moses, and get her to go and bring their dear ones away," he wrote. "How strange! This woman—one of the most ordinary looking of her race; unlettered, no idea of geography, asleep half of the time. . . . No fugitive was ever captured who had Moses for a leader."

Tubman was resourceful, courageous, and dedicated to freedom. But like the rest of the human race, she was also capable of making human errors. Apparently very lonely in her midthirties, she committed one of the strangest acts of her life: She abducted a child. The episode began in 1855 or 1856, when she stopped at the Eastern Shore home of one of her brothers and became captivated by his daughter Margaret. More than 80 years later, Margaret's daughter, then Mrs. A. J. Brickler of Wilberforce, Ohio, recounted the story to an interviewer:

> My mother's life really began with Aunt Harriet kidnapping her from her home on Eastern Shore, Maryland, when she was a little girl eight or nine years old. Aunt Harriet fell in love with the little girl who was my mother. Maybe it was because in mother she saw the child she herself might have been if slavery had been less cruel. Maybe it was because she knew the joys of motherhood would never be hers and she longed for some little creature who would love her for her own self's sake. Certainly whatever her emotion, it was stronger than her better judgment, for when her visit was ended, she, secretly, and without so much as a by-your-leave, took the little girl with her to her Northern home.

Tubman, continued her grandniece, "must have regretted her act for she knew she had taken the child from a sheltered good home to a place where there was nobody to care for her." In any event, said Brick-

William Henry Seward was governor of New York (1839–43), U.S. senator (1849–61), and U.S. secretary of state (1861–69). He was also one of Tubman's staunchest admirers. "I have known her long," he once wrote, "and a nobler, higher spirit, or a truer, seldom dwells in the human form."

ler, not long after she had carried Margaret off, Tubman "thought of her white friends . . . and decided to place her dearest possession in their hands." She brought Margaret to her friend Frances Seward, wife of U.S. senator William H. Seward. (A former governor of New York and a dedicated abolitionist, Seward would serve as U.S. secretary of state from 1861 until 1869.)

"This kindly lady," said Brickler, "brought up mother, not as a servant but as a guest within her home. She taught mother to speak properly, to read, write, sew, do housework, and act as a lady. Whenever Aunt Harriet came back, mother was dressed and sent in the Seward carriage to visit her. Strange to say, mother looked very much like Aunt Harriet."

In 1857, soon after her short-lived experience as a mother, Tubman settled down in a home of her own. She had always been forthright about asking supporters to help finance her rescue missions, but she never asked for personal funds. Now, however, her friend William Seward took a firm stand. According to biographer Bradford, he said, "Harriet, you have worked for others long enough," and presented her with the deed to a little house in Auburn, New York. To avoid any appearance of charity, Seward "sold" Tubman the house; he required no cash but asked her to make a regular series of small payments. Situated in the central part of the state, Auburn served as a major station on the Underground Railroad. The small town was to be Tubman's home for the rest of her life.

Not long after she moved to Auburn, Tubman received troubling news. Her father had been arrested and was awaiting trial for helping a fellow slave escape. In the eyes of the South, Ben Ross's crime was enormous; Tubman knew that even though he was more than 70 years old, he would be punished severely if found guilty. She made plans to head south immediately. Needing money for her trip, she stopped off at the New York City office of the Anti-Slavery Society and asked for $20, a sizable amount in 1857.

Tubman later told Sarah Bradford what happened next. The abolitionist official said, "*Twenty dollars! Who told you to come here for twenty dollars?*" Tubman replied, "The Lord told me, sir." "Well," countered the official, "I guess the Lord's mistaken this time." Tubman lifted her chin. "No, sir," she said, "the Lord's never mistaken! Anyhow, I'm going to sit here until I get it."

As good as her word, Tubman sat down and immediately went to sleep, probably suffering one of her frequent blackouts. As she slept and woke, then slept again, she was aware of visitors coming and going through the office. Many must have been sympathetic to her plight; when she awoke late in the afternoon, she found a pile of bills—amounting to $60—in her lap. Tubman set off for the Eastern Shore. Her father's trial was imminent, and there was no time to spare.

Tubman's rescue of her parents was a model of simplicity—and extraordinary daring. Slipping into Ben and Rit's cabin late one night, she told the as-

After rescuing her elderly parents from Maryland, Tubman brought them to this house in Auburn, New York. The building, purchased on easy terms from William Seward in 1857 and still standing today, was Tubman's home for more than 50 years.

tonished old people to prepare for a trip north. Next, she walked over to the plantation stable, found a horse, and hitched it to a rickety farm wagon. Then, wrote Quaker Thomas Garrett later, "She got her parents . . . on this rude vehicle . . . and drove to town in a style that no human being ever did before or since." Three days later, Tubman and her parents arrived in Wilmington. "I furnished her with money to take them all to Canada," wrote Garrett. "I afterward sold their horse and sent them the balance of the proceeds."

Tubman brought her parents first to Canada, then to Auburn. "Harriet's abduction of her parents was an event in Underground annals," observed biographer Earl Conrad in his 1943 account of Tubman. "It was significant, not only because rarely did aged folks take to the Road, but because Harriet carried them off with an audaciousness and an aplomb that represented complete mastery of the Railroad and perfect scorn of the white patrol. Her performance was that, at once, of the accomplished artist and the daring revolutionary."

Not everyone, however, applauded Tubman's courage. John Bell Robinson, a Philadelphia supporter of slavery, characterized the rescue of Ben and Rit as "a diabolical act of wickedness and cruelty." In his 1860 book, *Pictures of Slavery and Freedom*, Robinson called "the bringing away from ease and comfortable homes two old slaves over seventy years of age . . . as cruel an act as ever was performed by a child towards parents." To help elderly people to freedom was "a thousand times worse than to sell young ones away," insisted Robinson. Even "confinement in the penitentiary for life," he said, "would be inadequate to [Tubman's] crime." There is no indication that Tubman ever heard of Robinson or his opinions. If she did, perhaps she just looked at her parents and smiled.

By now, as Conrad observed, the Eastern Shore was being "plucked of slaves like a chicken of its feathers before roasting." And Harriet Tubman was the primary culprit. She began arming the runaways she sent north: In 1857, for example, she equipped a departing group of 28 men, women, and children with revolvers, pistols, and butcher knives. All of them made it safely to the home of Thomas Garrett and then to Canada. Frantic plantation owners hired more slave hunters and raised the price on Tubman's head. "It now came to pass," noted a contemporary northern account, "that . . . rewards were offered for the apprehension of the Negro woman who was denuding the fields of their laborers and the cabins of their human livestock."

In the late 1850s, Tubman agreed to speak at a few New England antislavery meetings. She had little time for such activities; between her trips south, she

Their stolen wagon hitched to a pair of oxen, a band of fugitives crosses Virginia's Rappahannock River. As Tubman brought more and more slaves out of the South, slave owners became increasingly eager to catch the woman who was "denuding the fields of their laborers."

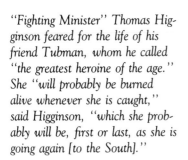

"Fighting Minister" Thomas Higginson feared for the life of his friend Tubman, whom he called "the greatest heroine of the age." She "will probably be burned alive whenever she is caught," said Higginson, "which she probably will be, first or last, as she is going again [to the South]."

had to work hard to support herself and her parents. (Strange as it seems, this daring commando earned her living as a domestic, usually in hotels.) When she did find time to address conventions, Tubman enthralled her audiences.

Clergyman Thomas Wentworth Higginson, president of the Massachusetts Anti-Slavery Society, often praised Tubman's abilities as a speaker. A celebrated orator himself, he said he had learned the art from "the slave women who had been stripped and whipped and handled with insolent hands and sold to the highest bidder . . . or women who, having once escaped, had, like Harriet Tubman, gone back again and again into the land of bondage to bring away their kindred and friends. . . . [I] learned to speak," he added, "because their presence made silence impossible."

Higginson, who was known as the Fighting Minister, wrote a letter to his mother about Tubman in 1859:

> We have had the greatest heroine of the age here, Harriet Tubman, a black woman and a fugitive slave. . . . Her tales of adventure are beyond anything in fiction and her ingenuity and generalship are extraordinary. . . . The slaves call her Moses. She has had a reward of twelve thousand dollars offered for her in Maryland and will probably be burned alive whenever she is caught, which she probably will be, first or last, as she is going again.

Despite her friend's grim predictions, Tubman was never caught. Before she changed her antislavery strategy, she would have made 19 excursions into the South, "stealing" more than 300 human beings from the land that had tried—and failed—to keep her in bondage.

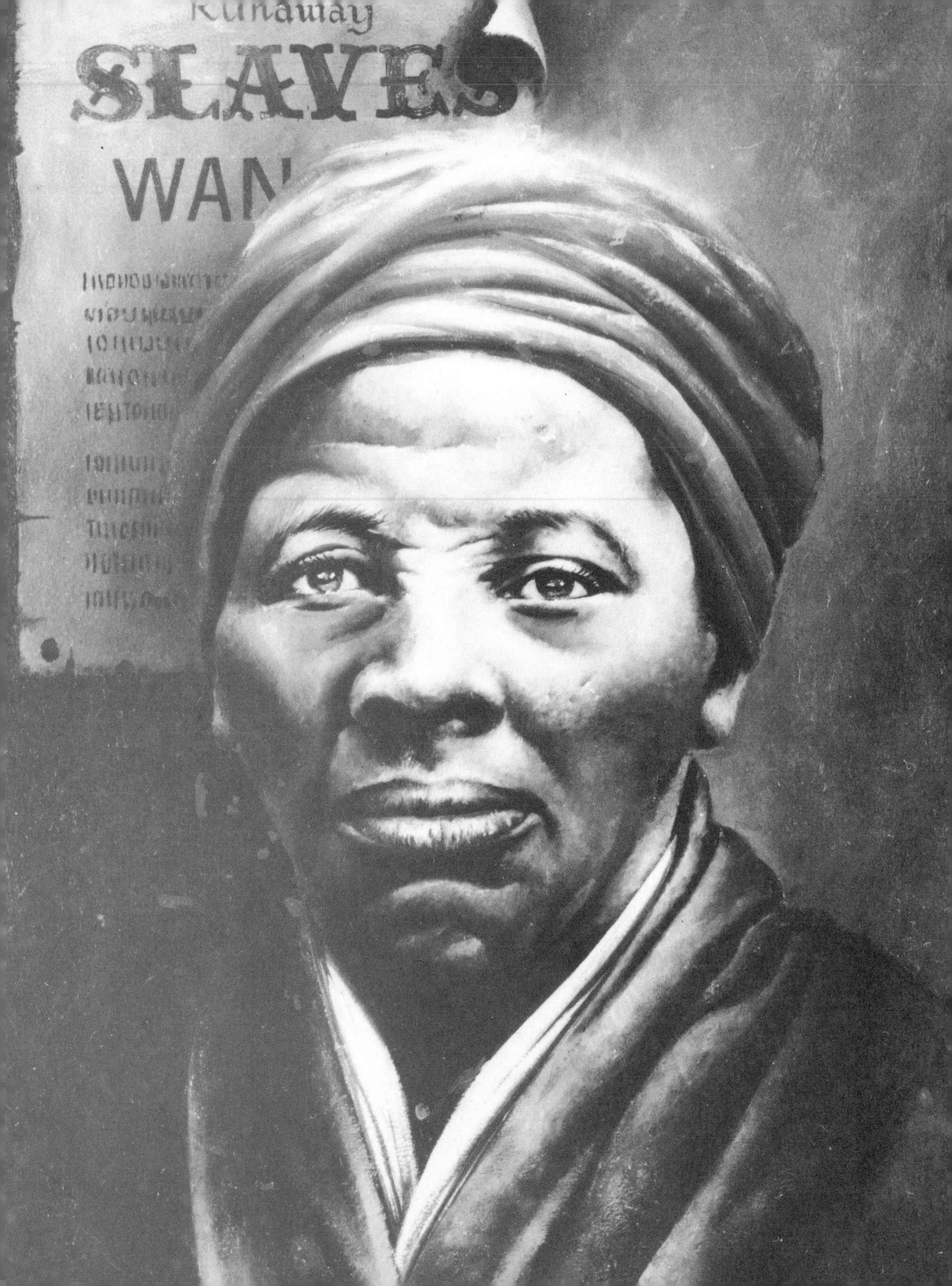
Runaway
SLAVES
WAN

7

GENERAL TUBMAN
GOES TO WAR

❧

HARRIET TUBMAN'S WORK had always involved stealth and secrecy; she chose, as Frederick Douglass once put it, "to labor in a private way," her activities observed only by "the midnight sky and the silent stars." She addressed occasional meetings only because her abolitionist friends insisted; a few words from her, they said, helped the cause more than dozens of speeches by its educated, well-to-do supporters. After she caught the attention of John Brown, however, Tubman lost any chance for obscurity.

Convinced he was God's instrument to destroy slavery, Brown had already battled proslavery forces in Kansas. By the late 1850s, he had decided it was time to take arms and end slavery everywhere. For his starting point, he settled on a little town at the northernmost corner of the South. He would assemble an army of abolitionists, both black and white, and strike at Harpers Ferry, Virginia, where the Potomac River passes through a gap in the Blue Ridge Mountains.

Brown planned to bring weapons to Harpers Ferry, seize more arms from the town's large arsenal, then retreat to the mountains, where he expected thousands of rebellious slaves to join him. With these

Tubman, probably about 40 years old in this portrait, still bears a scar on her temple from the ferocious blow she had received as a teenager. She also continued to suffer from the unpredictable "sleeping fits" induced by her near-fatal head wound.

John Brown, who believed he had a divine mission to end slavery by force, became a national figure during the Kansas Territory slavery battles of the mid-1850s. By the end of the decade, he was ready to start a full-scale war.

troops behind him, Brown expected to liberate all the slaves in the South, then establish a new national government. By late 1857, he had recruited a small band of free blacks and fugitive slaves. What he needed now was black leadership—charismatic figures who could inspire and lead these volunteers. He believed there were two such leaders in the United States: Harriet Tubman and Frederick Douglass. Brown would invite them both to join him in his great enterprise.

In the spring of 1858, Brown traveled through New England, rounding up support for his revolution among such leading abolitionists as Thomas Higginson and Franklin Sanborn of Massachusetts. From New England, Brown went on to New York State, meeting up with Frederick Douglass in Rochester. The celebrated orator, former slave, and abolitionist was apparently skeptical about Brown's plan, but he encouraged the fiery reformer to talk to Harriet Tubman, who had spent the winter working in St. Catharines. Accompanied by Tubman's friend, J. W. Loguen, the black clergyman and abolitionist, Brown accordingly headed for Canada. He arrived in April.

During the preceding winter, Tubman had had a recurring dream. Night after night, she recalled later, she dreamed of a "wilderness sort of place, all full of rocks and bushes." In the dream, a snake raised its head from among the rocks; as she watched, it turned into the head of an old man with a white beard and fierce, glittering eyes. He gazed at her, she said, "wishful like, just as if he was going to speak to me." Then, in the dream, two other heads, younger than the first, appeared. Finally, a crowd of men rushed in and struck down all three heads. Tubman told friends about the dream, which puzzled and disturbed her.

When she met John Brown, Tubman stared hard. His was the face—that of the old, bearded man with fire in his eyes—that she had seen in her dream. Still, the dream's meaning was unclear to her; maybe its message would reveal itself later. Meanwhile, Brown told Tubman of his planned revolution and asked her about the Underground Railroad, through which he hoped to channel slaves to join him at Harpers Ferry. He also asked her to recruit free blacks for the impending battle.

Clearly impressed with "General Tubman," as he called the militant black woman, Brown wrote a letter to his son about her. Curiously, he spoke of her as a man; perhaps he found it hard to believe that a woman could possess such strong qualities of leadership. "I came here direct with J. W. Loguen," said Brown's letter. "I am succeeding beyond my expectation. Harriet Tubman is the most of a man, naturally, that I ever met with. There is the most abundant material, and of the right quality, in this quarter, beyond all doubt."

During the following winter (1858–59), Tubman met with John Brown in Boston. There, the two conferred with Franklin Sanborn and other supporters of Brown's plan. Writing about that winter, Sanborn later noted that Brown "always spoke of [Tubman] with the greatest respect, and said that 'General Tubman,' as he styled her, was a better officer than most whom he had seen, and could command an army as successfully as she had led her small parties of fugitives."

Wendell Phillips, another great antislavery orator, met Tubman for the first time that winter. "The last time I ever saw John Brown," Phillips later recalled, "was under my own roof, as he brought Harriet Tubman to me, saying, 'Mr. Phillips, I bring you one of the best and bravest persons on this continent—General Tubman, as we call her.' "

Scheduled, delayed, and rescheduled several times, Brown's attack on Harpers Ferry would finally

Frederick Douglass shared John Brown's abolitionist goals, but he declined to join the old warrior's raid on Harpers Ferry, Virginia. "An attack on the federal government," Douglass warned Brown, "would array the whole country against us."

take place in October 1859. When the critical day arrived, however, Brown had neither of the black leaders he wanted at his side. Douglass, finally deciding that Brown's plan was doomed to failure, declined to join in the attack. Tubman, too, was absent.

Wholeheartedly admiring John Brown, Tubman had intended to join him for his historic battle. But in the summer of 1859, at the very moment she had planned to lend him her assistance, she fell ill. She had long suffered from the effects of the head wound she received as a young woman. Now almost 40, she found herself on the verge of exhaustion: The years of strenuous Underground Railroad journeys, combined with the heavy labor by which she supported herself and her parents, had caught up with her.

Tubman probably collapsed in Boston. In any case, friends took the sick woman to their home in New Bedford, Massachusetts, to recover. Meanwhile, Brown and his lieutenants had no idea where to find the "General," and she had no idea when the attack on Harpers Ferry would actually begin. In his biography of John Brown, the eminent black scholar W. E. B. Du Bois wrote, "Only sickness, brought on by her toil and exposure, prevented Harriet from being present at Harpers Ferry."

On the night of October 16, 1859, John Brown led his little band of abolitionist militants into the Virginia town and seized its federal arsenal. At his side were 5 blacks and 16 whites, 3 of them his sons. Almost immediately, Brown's fighters were attacked by citizens and local militia, who were soon joined by a company of United States Marines. With 10 of his men—including 2 of his sons—killed, Brown surrendered. Soon afterward, he was tried for treason, convicted, and hanged. Six of his remaining followers met the same fate.

When a horrified Tubman, still recovering from her illness, learned about the outcome of Brown's

raid, she must have recalled her dream of the previous winter; had those three stricken heads represented John Brown and his sons?

After Brown's trial, many abolitionists, including Tubman, kept as far away from the public eye as possible. They knew their names had been mentioned in the letters and papers that Brown had left scattered around the farmhouse from which he had staged his raid. Several prominent abolitionists, including Frederick Douglass, even left the country for a period. A Senate committee investigated the role played by the northern abolitionists, but in the end, none was accused of involvement in the Harpers Ferry raid. Tubman finally returned to her home in Auburn, still sick and now in mourning for the white man she had admired above all others of his race.

She must have been moved by Frederick Douglass's tribute to the slain visionary. "John Brown began the war that ended American slavery," said

Outnumbered and outgunned, John Brown's forces battle federal troops at the Harpers Ferry arsenal. Brown had hoped to enlist Tubman and Frederick Douglass in a mighty blow against slavery, but he went into action without either ally and with only 21 men behind him.

John Brown, a rope around his neck, heads for the gallows after his failed 1859 raid on Harpers Ferry. Devastated by the news of Brown's fate, Tubman said, "It was not John Brown that died. . . . It was Christ—it was the saviour of our people."

Douglass. "Until this blow was struck, the prospect for freedom was dim, shadowy, and uncertain. . . . When John Brown stretched forth his arm the sky was cleared—the armed hosts of freedom stood face to face over the chasm of a broken union, and the clash of arms was at hand."

By the following spring, Tubman was recovered and ready to renew her labors. In April, she staged her own raid, overwhelming scores of lawmen and rescuing fugitive slave Charles Nalle in Troy, New York. "Harriet Tubman's victory," commented biographer Earl Conrad, "was a high point of the fugitive slave history that racked the nation's breast for 10 years. If Brown's Virginia raid was a dress rehearsal for the Civil War, Harriet's action was a bugle call for the war to begin."

From Troy, Tubman went on to Boston. There, her friend and fellow Harpers Ferry conspirator, Frank Sanborn, escorted her from one gathering of social activists to another. She met many of the Bostonians passionately concerned with abolition, woman suffrage, economic theory, human rights, and civic reform. In a city preoccupied with the rights of women and blacks, Harriet Tubman became a highly sought-after speaker.

In drawing rooms all over Boston, men and women listened raptly as Tubman talked about her days as a slave, her travels on the Underground Railroad, and her association with the martyred John Brown. At one point, she said, "It was not John Brown that died at Charles Town [the Virginia town where he was hanged]. *It was Christ*—it was the saviour of our people."

Much of the talk in Boston revolved around the possibilities of ending slavery peacefully. Attired, as usual, in a well-worn gray cotton dress, its neck trimmed with lace and its full skirt reaching the floor, Tubman listened to such hopes silently but skeptically. At one point, Sanborn later recalled, she leaned toward him and whispered, "They may say, 'Peace, Peace!' as much as they like; I know there's going to be war!"

In Boston, Tubman spent most of her time with abolitionist groups, but she did make one speech at a women's rights convention, organized in 1860 by celebrated suffragists Susan B. Anthony and Elizabeth Cady Stanton. No record remains of Tubman's words, but a contemporary observer, author Robert W. Taylor, reported on their effects. "She made the weak strong, the strong determined, and the determined invincible," said Taylor. "After her words of untutored but fiery eloquence, her hearers stood like Martin Luther of old, body and soul and spirit devoted singly and untiringly to one end."

But for a woman of action, only so much time could be spent in drawing rooms and convention halls. As it happened, events in the fall of 1860 would plunge Tubman back into the tumultuous South. In November, Abraham Lincoln was elected president. Appalled by the victory of an abolitionist, South Carolina quickly seceded from the Union, virtually guaranteeing the flight of the rest of the cotton states. The specter of civil war loomed closer. Tubman, realizing that war would make it harder than ever to bring slaves out of the South, decided to make another foray into the Tidewater.

Supplied with traveling money by Boston abolitionists, Tubman headed for Maryland, where she picked up five slaves: Maria and Stephen Ennets and their three children, one of them a three-month-old baby. On her way north, Tubman collected two additional passengers, a man and a woman.

In December, Thomas Garrett of Wilmington sent a note to William Still of the Philadelphia Vigilance Committee. "I write to let thee know that Harriet Tubman is again in these parts. She arrived

By 1860, when he was elected president, Abraham Lincoln had made his position on slavery clear: "As I would not be a slave, so I would not be a master," he said in 1858. "This expresses my idea of democracy." Lincoln's election sparked South Carolina's secession from the Union and made civil war inevitable.

last evening from one of her trips of mercy to God's poor. . . . I gave Harriet ten dollars, to hire a man with a carriage to take them to [Philadelphia]. . . . I shall be very uneasy about them till I hear they are safe. There is now much more risk on the road . . . yet, as it is Harriet, who seems to have had a special angel to guard her on her journeys of mercy, I have hope."

The fugitives reached Philadelphia safely, and Still recorded their arrival in his book. Having learned from John Brown's mistakes, however, Still was now keeping less-detailed notes. The capture of Brown's letters and papers, he wrote, "with names and plans in full, admonished us that such papers and correspondence as had been preserved concerning the Underground Rail Road, might perchance be captured by a pro-slavery mob."

Tubman's 1860 Railroad trip was her last, although not by her own choice. As the North-South split widened, the South clamored ever more loudly for enforcement of the Fugitive Slave Act and for punishment of anyone who broke it. "Those anxious months, when darkness settled over our political prospects, were viewed by all classes with deep forebodings," Frank Sanborn recalled later. The times, said Sanborn, were especially dangerous "for those who, like Harriet, had rendered themselves obnoxious to the supporters of slavery by running off so many of their race from its dominions. Fear for her personal safety caused Harriet's friends to hurry her off to Canada, sorely against her will."

But Tubman was not to stay long in Canadian safety. In February 1861, the remaining six states of the Deep South (Alabama, Florida, Georgia, Louisiana, Mississippi, and Texas) withdrew from the Union to form the Confederate States of America. On April 12, Confederate troops opened fire on the federal garrison at Fort Sumter in Charleston, South

Confederate officers drive slaves away from approaching Union troops. Despite the rebels' efforts, thousands of blacks remained in South Carolina, flooding Union army bases in the Sea Islands and forcing overwhelmed commanders to call for civilian assistance. Heeding the call, Tubman headed south in 1862.

Carolina. The fort surrendered on April 13, and the nation went to war.

As Union troops advanced through Maryland in the spring and summer of 1861, large numbers of blacks left their plantations to join the northern soldiers. Officially called "contraband of war," these blacks were no longer slaves but were not yet legally free; Lincoln would not sign his Emancipation Proclamation, liberating the slaves of the South, until January 1, 1863.

In April 1861, when she learned that the federal armies needed help in caring for the "contrabands," Tubman headed south. Little is known of her activities during this period, but according to historian William Wells Brown, she remained on "the outskirts of the Union Army" until the fall, "doing good service for those of her people who sought protection in the Union lines."

Tubman was back in Auburn with her elderly parents when Union forces took Port Royal in South Carolina's Sea Islands. Plantation owners fled the islands for the mainland, leaving thousands of their slaves behind. These contrabands, many of them illiterate, malnourished and ill, flooded the Union army camps. Overwhelmed by this human tide, Union army commanders sent out a call for teachers

Newly released slaves line up outside a contraband school. Adding to their other problems, the contrabands around Beaufort spoke an African-flavored language that few outsiders—including Tubman—could understand.

and nurses. Hundreds of northerners responded; among them, not surprisingly, was Harriet Tubman.

Arriving at Beaufort, South Carolina, in March 1862, Tubman discovered that she could barely communicate with the local black people. Still linked closely to Africa—the last (illegal) slave ship had delivered its cargo to the area in 1849—these former slaves spoke a dialect called Gullah, which contained many African words. "Why, their language down there in the far South," Tubman later told Sarah Bradford, "is just as different from ours in Maryland as you can think. They laughed when they heard me talk, and I could not understand them."

Adding to the language problem was suspicion. These blacks of the Deep South had little trust for whites or those who worked for them. Isolated on their offshore islands, they had never heard of Moses or the Underground Railroad. Tubman, assigned to the contraband hospital, had to win her patients' confidence step by step. She was entitled to army rations and supplies, but when she learned that the contrabands were jealous of her privileges, she gave them up. To supply her personal needs, she sold pies and root beer, which she made at night, after working in the hospital all day.

While she was in Beaufort, Tubman dictated a letter to her friend Frank Sanborn. In it, she described her patients as "very destitute, almost naked." She said, "I am trying to find places for those able to work, and provide for them as best I can, so as to lighten the burden of the Government as much as possible, while at the same time they learn to respect themselves by earning their own living."

Tubman nursed both the blacks who poured into Beaufort and white soldiers injured in the field. It was sometimes discouraging work. Years later, she described it to Sarah Bradford:

> I'd go to the hospital early every morning. I'd get a big chunk of ice and put it in a basin, and fill it with water; then I'd take a sponge and begin. First man I'd come to, I'd thrash away the flies, and they'd rise, like bees around a hive. Then I'd begin to bathe their wounds, and by the time I'd bathed off three or four [soldiers], the fire and heat would have melted the ice and made the water warm, and it would be as red as clear blood. Then I'd go and get more ice, and by the time I got to the next one, the flies would be around the first ones black and thick as ever.

Although she could not read them, Tubman kept many of the notes and orders she received at Beaufort. One note, addressed by a hospital surgeon to the base commissary, reveals the lack of supplies available to Tubman and other medical workers. "Will Captain Warfield," read the note, "please let 'Moses' have a little Bourbon whiskey for medicinal purposes."

Tubman worked at several southern locations, reporting when she was needed, then moving on. "'Moses' was in her glory," wrote historian William Wells Brown, "and travelled from camp to camp, being always treated in the most respectful manner. The black men would have died for this woman."

From Beaufort, Tubman went to a military hospital in Fernandina, Florida. There, she later re-

As a Civil War nurse in South Carolina, Tubman worked in this Beaufort manor house, converted into a hospital for contrabands. Eager to teach these impoverished and homeless people "to respect themselves," Tubman not only cared for the sick but helped find jobs for the healthy.

When Tubman ran into her old friend Thomas Higginson in 1862, he was commanding the all-black 1st South Carolina Volunteers. Deeply impressed by his men's fighting abilities, Higginson told the War Department that "the successful prosecution of the war lies in the unlimited employment of black troops."

ported, soldiers were "dying off like sheep" from dysentery. When she discovered no medicine to treat them, Tubman searched the woods for certain roots; these she used to treat the men, achieving remarkable results in many cases. She also nursed soldiers and contrabands stricken with smallpox and "malignant fevers," or malaria. Despite her willing exposure to these highly contagious diseases, Tubman never contracted one herself. "The Lord would take care of me," she told Bradford, "until my time came."

Back in Beaufort in December 1862, Tubman heard a bit of interesting news. Her old friend Thomas Higginson was at nearby Camp Saxton, where he was organizing a regiment of black soldiers. In a letter to his wife, dated December 10, Higginson wrote: "Who should drive out to see me today but Harriet Tubman who is living at Beaufort as a sort of nurse & general care taker; she sends her regards to you. All sorts of unexpected people turn up here."

Tubman's days as a "general care taker," however, were drawing to a close. Among the needs of the Union army in South Carolina was information: Where were the enemy encampments? How many men did they have? How well were they armed? Aware of her work on the Underground Railroad, Union officers assigned Tubman to a new job: spy. In the spring of 1863, she organized a scouting service, leading a small band of black men deep into enemy territory and returning with information on Confederate movements. She reported to Colonel James Montgomery, an expert in guerrilla warfare who had fought at the side of John Brown in Kansas.

Perhaps the most celebrated of Tubman's military exploits took place in the summer of 1863. Deciding the time was ripe for a raid up South Carolina's Combahee River, General David Hunter, commander of the Union's southern forces, called on Harriet Tubman. Her mission: to take "several gunboats up the

Combahee River, the object of the expedition being to take up the torpedoes [mines] placed by the rebels on the river, to destroy railroads and bridges, and to cut off supplies and troops." Hunter also wanted Tubman to lead out the hundreds of blacks known to be in the Confederate-held area. Tubman accepted the assignment.

On the night of June 2, 1863, she and Colonel Montgomery started up the river with a force of 150 black soldiers in 3 steam-powered gunboats. The expedition, as the Boston *Commonwealth* later reported, "dashed into the enemy's country, struck a bold and effective blow, destroying millions of dollars worth of commissary stores, cotton, and lordly dwellings, and striking terror into the heart of rebeldom, brought off near 800 slaves and thousands of dollars worth of property, without losing a man or receiving a scratch."

Aware that the spectacular raid had been led by a black woman, humiliated Confederate commanders chose to blame their defeat on one of their own officers. "On this occasion," said the official Confederate report, "[the officer's] pickets were neither watchful nor brave; they allowed . . . a parcel of negro wretches, calling themselves soldiers, with a

Confederate soldiers and their dogs attack a black South Carolina regiment. Black fighting men faced double jeopardy: they could be killed on the field, or they could be taken prisoner and murdered by rebel soldiers, who refused to treat them as legitimate prisoners of war.

few degraded whites, to march unmolested, with the incendiary torch, to rob, destroy and burn a large section of the country."

Tubman knew that Colonel Montgomery, the white officer technically in command of the Combahee raid, would get most of the credit for its success. Ordinarily self-effacing, she allowed herself a touch of defensive pride on this occasion. In a letter she dictated to Frank Sanborn, she said:

> You have without a doubt seen a full account of the expedition. Don't you think we colored people are entitled to some of the credit for that exploit, under the lead of the brave Colonel Montgomery? We weakened the rebels somewhat on the Combahee River, by taking and bringing away *seven hundred and fifty-six* head of their most valuable live stock, known up in your region as "contrabands," and this, too, without the loss of a single life on our part, though we had good reason to believe a number of rebels bit the dust. Of those seven hundred and fifty-six contrabands, nearly or quite all the able-bodied men have joined the colored regiments here.

In the same letter, Tubman said, "I have now been absent two years, almost. . . . My father and

A trio of "contrabands"—southern blacks no longer slaves but not yet legally free—reports to a Union officer and his staff. At first regarded with suspicion by the northern military, contraband volunteers proved able and willing recruits.

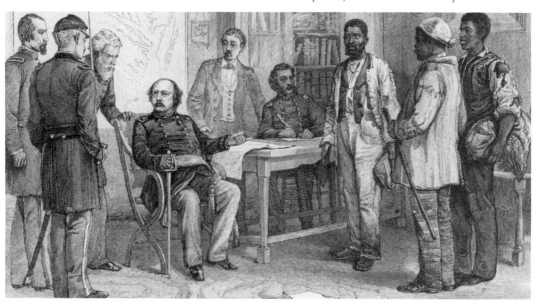

The 54th Massachusetts storms the parapet of Fort Wagner, in Charleston, South Carolina. Tubman probably saw the attack, which, observed the New York Tribune, "made Fort Wagner such a name to the colored race as Bunker Hill [Boston's revolutionary war battle site] had been for 90 years to the Yankees."

mother are old and in feeble health, and need my care and attention. I hope the good people [in Auburn] will not allow them to suffer, and I do not believe that they will. But I do not see how I am to leave at present the very important work to be done here."

Tubman would continue to perform that important work until the war ended, almost two years later. During that time, she would see some of the bloodiest battles of the Civil War. Among them was the celebrated Union assault on Fort Wagner, a Confederate bastion that guarded the harbor of Charleston, South Carolina. Leading the July 18, 1863, attack on Fort Wagner was the 54th Massachusetts, a black infantry regiment led by a 26-year-old white officer, Colonel Robert Gould Shaw. The battle marked the first important use of black troops, whose courage under fire was doubted by many whites, northerners as well as southerners.

Advancing through a murderous hail of shot and shell, the regiment captured Wagner's parapet, but

The men of Company E, 4th U.S. Colored Infantry Volunteers, prepare for inspection in 1865. President Lincoln vigorously supported the use of blacks in the army: "Abandon all the posts now possessed by black men," he said in 1864, "and we would be compelled to abandon the war in three weeks."

in the end, the entrenched Confederate position held. The 54th lost the battle, its young commander, and about half its men, but it demonstrated the extraordinary courage of its black soldiers. Their valor, however, failed to impress the South: When Colonel Shaw's father later asked for the return of his son's body, Confederate officers refused. "We have buried him," they said, "with his niggers."

But Fort Wagner transformed the North's view of the black fighting man. "Through the cannon smoke of that dark night," observed the *Atlantic Monthly*, "the manhood of the colored race shines before many eyes that would not see." After Fort Wagner, black soldiers fought on all fronts, with no one expressing doubts about their courage or ability.

Tubman probably witnessed the South Carolina battle. The night before, she served Shaw his dinner, and the next day, she helped bury the dead and nurse the wounded. Years later, she told historian Albert Bushnell Hart about a Civil War engagement that may have been Fort Wagner:

And then we saw the lightning, and that was the guns; and then we heard the thunder, and that was the big guns; and then we heard the rain falling, and that was the drops of blood falling; and when we came to get in the crops, it was dead men that we reaped.

For the next year, Tubman remained in the South. Taking part in numerous guerrilla operations, she earned respectful admiration from the military, foot soldiers and officers alike. As General Rufus Saxton, a Union officer responsible for organizing contraband regiments, later put it, "She made many a raid inside the enemy's lines, displaying remarkable courage, zeal, and fidelity." ✺

8

"THIS HEROIC WOMAN"

Her face reflecting years of hardship and exhausting labor, Tubman sits for an Auburn photographer in the late 1860s. Despite her heroic war work as a nurse, spy, scout, and commando, Tubman never received a penny from the United States government.

IN MAY 1864, Harriet Tubman applied for leave from her duties at the Port Royal military hospital. Her boss, surgeon Henry Durrant, approved her request and gave her a note of reference. "I certify that I have been acquainted with Harriet Tubman for nearly two years," read the note, which Tubman saved. "My position as Medical Officer in charge of 'contrabands' in [Beaufort] has given me frequent and ample opportunities to observe her general deportment; particularly her kindness and attention to the sick and suffering of her own race. I take much pleasure in testifying to the esteem in which she is generally held." At the bottom of the note was a line signed by General Saxton: "I concur fully in the above."

Eager to see her aged parents, Tubman headed for Auburn, New York. Once there, her years of nonstop wartime service seemed to catch up with her; exhausted and ill, she suffered an intense bout of the sleeping seizures that had long plagued her. She spent almost a year in Auburn, resting and quietly visiting friends and neighbors. It was during this period that Tubman met and became friends with Sarah Bradford, the white woman from Geneva, New York, who was to become her first biographer.

A northern conductor orders a black passenger out of a postwar whites-only railroad car. Although the North had fought to free the South's slaves, Tubman and other blacks soon discovered that northern whites could be as bigoted as their southern counterparts.

By the early spring of 1865, Tubman felt well enough to return to the war. She set out for South Carolina, but by the time she reached Washington, D.C., a string of Union victories indicated that the war would soon be over. Tubman decided to remain in the Washington area, where she worked as a nurse for the U.S. Sanitary Commission, that era's equivalent of the Medical Corps.

On April 9, Confederate general Robert E. Lee surrendered to U.S. general Ulysses S. Grant at Appomattox, Virginia. A few months later, a weary Harriet Tubman once again turned her eyes toward Auburn and home. The Civil War was over. But for Tubman and millions of other free black Americans, another war had just begun.

Carrying a half-fare military pass, Tubman boarded a northbound train in Washington. The white conductor who looked at the pass refused to honor it. Tubman later told Bradford the story. "Come, hustle out of here!" shouted the conductor. "Niggers," he said, were not entitled to travel at reduced rates. When she protested, he grabbed her arm and said, "I'll make you tired of trying to stay here." With three other men, the conductor then dragged her out of the passenger car. The train's white passengers watched in silence. No one came to Tubman's aid as her four burly assailants wrestled her along to the baggage car and literally threw her in.

Tubman rode north alone, cradling a severely sprained arm. She rarely complained about anything, but she must have noted the incident's bitter irony. Harriet Tubman, the woman who had led troops in battle for the Union, the daring rescuer who had escaped bullets, bloodhounds, and angry slave owners, had suffered her first war injury from a civilian in the "free" North.

Although Tubman had been entitled to military pay for her services as a scout and nurse, she had never demanded it—and never received it. In 1864, the Boston *Commonwealth* had called attention to this injustice. "This heroic woman," said the newspaper, "[and] her services to her people and to the army seem to have been inadequately recompensed by the military authorities, and such money as she has received, she has expended for others as her custom is."

Tubman had carefully saved her receipts and records from the war years. Using these documents, Tubman's friends concluded that the United States government owed her $1,800 for her military services. When her own requests for payment went unheeded, Tubman's old friend William H. Seward, now secretary of state, along with such influential allies as Colonel Thomas Higginson and General Rufus Saxton, petitioned Congress in her behalf. "I can bear witness to the value of her services in South Carolina and Florida," wrote Saxton. "She was employed in the hospitals and as a spy . . . and is as deserving of a pension from the government for her services as any other of its faithful servants."

Tubman desperately needed the money to support herself and her parents and to continue helping others. Astonishingly, nothing happened; Tubman's special case, it seemed, came under no official law. In one session after another, an indifferent postwar Congress refused to recognize the rights of this black woman who had worked and fought for her country. The debt was never paid.

When Tubman returned to Auburn, she was about 45 years old, penniless, and responsible for 2 aged parents. She was also in steady pain from the arm the trainmen had savagely wrenched. Nevertheless, she went about her affairs with her customary verve. She planted apple trees and broke ground for a large vegetable garden to feed her family and those who came to her door. With the help of well-to-do

Former slaves work at a county poorhouse. Determined to keep as many blacks as she could from such a disheartening life, Tubman resolved to open a home where the sick and elderly could find health care, companionship, and peace.

neighbors, she established a kind of refuge for the many impoverished blacks who passed through the area in search of work and homes. She fed them, nursed their sick, and helped deliver their babies. Apparently with strength to spare, Tubman also began a fund-raising campaign to support schools for newly freed blacks in the South.

Tubman's good-humored energy may have flagged in October 1867, when a friend sent her a clipping from the *Baltimore American*. Asking a neighbor to read it to her, Tubman learned that her former husband was dead. John Tubman, the satisfied free black man who had once threatened to betray his wife for running away, had been shot down in broad daylight by a white man. Although John Tubman had been unarmed, and although witnesses testified to the cold-blooded killing, an all-white postwar Maryland jury had found the white man not guilty. Harriet Tubman's reaction to the news can only be guessed; she never said a word about it.

Meanwhile, she was finding it increasingly hard to make ends meet. Sarah Bradford illustrated the black woman's plight with an anecdote about the winter of 1867–68. A blizzard had all but buried Tubman's little house on the outskirts of Auburn, preventing her from working or going out for food. "At length," wrote Bradford, "stern necessity compelled her to plunge through the drifts to the city." Calling on "one of her firm and fast friends," Tubman "began to walk up and down, as she always [did] when in trouble." Her eyes filled with tears, Tubman seemed unable to speak. Finally, "with a great effort, she said, 'Miss Annie, could you lend me a quarter till Monday? I never asked it before.' Kind friends immediately supplied all the wants of the family, but on Monday Harriet appeared with the quarter she had borrowed."

At about this time, Bradford began writing her biography. First printed in 1869 under the title *Scenes in the Life of Harriet Tubman*, the book carried a slightly apologetic preface by Bradford. "There are those who will sneer, there are those who have already done so, at this quixotic [impractical] attempt to make a heroine of a black woman, and a slave," she observed. Nevertheless, with financial aid from Wendell Phillips and other friends, Bradford published the book, then turned its proceeds—some $1,200—over to its subject. A considerable sum for the time, the money allowed Tubman to pay her expenses, continue to support southern schools for blacks, and feed the hungry strangers at her door.

Appearing at her door in 1869 was another kind of visitor: a tall, handsome man named Nelson Davis. Some years earlier, in 1864, Tubman had met him at a South Carolina army base. Davis, then about 20 years old, was a private in Company G of the 8th U.S. Colored Infantry Volunteers. Whether Davis came to Auburn in search of Tubman or by chance is unknown; what is known is that the former soldier asked the former spy to marry him. Despite their age difference—Davis was at least 24 years younger than Tubman—she accepted.

Surrounded by friends, both black and white, the couple married on March 18, 1869. The next day, the Auburn newspaper reported on the ceremony. "Before a large and very select audience Harriet Tubman . . . took unto herself a husband and made one [Nelson Davis] a happy man," noted the paper. "Both born slaves . . . they stood there, last evening, *free*, and were joined as man and wife."

By all accounts, the good-looking Davis seemed unusually robust, but his appearance belied the truth. He had contracted tuberculosis in the army, and his health was fragile. Some people believed that Tubman, ever the care giver, married him so she could nurse him. In any case, Davis apparently never worked during the 19 years of his marriage.

Among the guests at Tubman and Davis's wedding had been William H. Seward. He and Tubman had not agreed on every issue (Seward had, for example, never supported Harriet's idol, John Brown), but the two remained staunch friends for decades. Seward was to die only a few years later, in 1872; at his funeral, hundreds of people passed his casket and the mountains of elaborate floral displays surrounding it. When the service ended, mourners saw a small black woman walk to the casket and lay a wreath of wildflowers at its foot.

The years were carrying away Tubman's most cherished possessions, the people she loved. She lost her parents, both nearing 100 years of age, in the 1870s. Quaker Thomas Garrett of Wilmington died in 1869, Colonel James Montgomery (Tubman's col-

Tubman's shawl hangs from the bed where she slept in her later years. Her Auburn house was small and sparsely furnished, but it was palatial compared to the ditches and "potato holes" in which she had stayed during her Underground Railroad days.

league on the Combahee raid) in 1871, Wendell Phillips in 1884, Frederick Douglass in 1895. By the 1890s, of all the thundering abolitionist band, only Thomas Higginson, Frank Sanborn, and Harriet Tubman lived on.

Tubman never changed: Needy people could always count on a meal or a place to stay when they came to her door. She dreamed of building a home for the poor and helpless, but the closing decades of the century were lean times, even for this gritty, resourceful woman.

In severe need of money, Tubman fell prey to a pair of black swindlers who came to Auburn in 1873. The men told her they had found a chest in the South containing $5,000 in gold. They said they did not want to exchange the gold for greenbacks (U.S. dollars) because the government would seize the gold and leave them penniless. If Tubman could raise

$2,000 in cash, the men said, they would turn the chest over to her. Tubman, who had seen such treasures hidden away by slaveholders, believed the story and persuaded friends to back her with $2,000. She agreed to meet the swindlers in the woods on a dark night: There, they knocked her unconscious, took the cash, and vanished. The episode became something of a scandal, but Auburn's citizens, even those who had lost their money, soon forgave Tubman. They knew she had been as much a victim as themselves.

In these years, Tubman earned her living as a peddler, traveling from house to house and selling vegetables from her garden. Neighbors welcomed her, eager to hear stories about her days on the Underground Railroad and her wartime activities. One of these friends later recalled: "Harriet when I knew her in her matriarchal phase was a magnificent looking woman, true African, with a broad nose, very black, and of medium height. I used to often sit and listen to her stories when I could get her to tell them. We always gave her something to eat. She preferred butter in her tea to anything else. That was a luxury."

In 1890, 2 years after her husband, Nelson Davis, died at the age of 44, Tubman finally got enough money to buy a few such "luxuries" herself: Congress approved pensions for the widows of Civil War veterans. Ironically, the government allotted Tubman $8 per month (increased to $20 in 1899) as the survivor of a soldier, but it steadfastly refused to reward her for her own gallant service.

Although her own government never recognized her, Great Britain's ruler did. After reading Bradford's biography of Tubman in 1897, a clearly impressed Queen Victoria had sent the American woman a silver medal and a letter inviting her to come to England. She never went, but her friends later reported that Tubman looked at the letter so many times, it "was worn to a shadow." The former slave had never forgotten her 1856 trip to Canada, when she had ushered the despairing Joe Bailey into "Queen Victoria's dominions" and freedom.

Another woman long admired by Tubman was Susan B. Anthony. Tubman had heard the great suffragist speak on a number of occasions, and she wholeheartedly endorsed Anthony's goals. Anthony, who returned Tubman's respect, referred to her fellow activist as "this most wonderful woman." Late in her life, Tubman received a visit from Elizabeth Miller, leader of a local suffragist group. Miller later described the occasion. "I remember seeing you years ago at a suffragist convention in Rochester," she told Tubman. "Yes," responded Tubman, "I belonged to Miss Susan B. Anthony's organization." Miller said she would like to enroll Tubman as a life member in her group. "You certainly have assisted in bearing the burdens," Miller continued. "Do you really believe that women should vote?" Tubman paused. Then she said softly, "I suffered enough to believe it."

As Tubman grew older, she became increasingly determined to establish a home for sick and needy black people. She had long had her eye on a 25-acre lot across the road from her house; the site, she thought, would be perfect for the poor people's shelter. In 1896, the property came up for public auction, and Tubman saw her chance. She had almost no money, but she had her usual supply of optimism and determination. She later told an interviewer about the auction:

> They were all white folks there but me, and I was there like a blackberry in a pail of milk, but I hid down in a corner, and no one knew who was bidding. The man began down pretty low, and I kept going up by fifties. At last I got up to fourteen hundred and fifty, and then others stopped bidding, and the man said, "All done. Who is the buyer?"
>
> "Harriet Tubman," I shouted.

Tubman left the astonished auction crowd and headed for the local bank, where she got the money

Women's rights activist Susan B. Anthony (left) confers with colleague Elizabeth Cady Stanton in 1900. Although Tubman focused most of her energies on abolition, she was also a strong supporter of Anthony and her suffragist movement. "Tell the women," she said a month before she died, "to stand together."

Tubman worshiped regularly at Auburn's African Methodist Episcopal Zion Church, where her strong, clear voice rang out in such favorite songs as "Swing Low, Sweet Chariot" and "Go Down, Moses." According to local reports, many parishioners attended the church as much to hear Tubman sing as for religious motives.

for her new land by mortgaging it (using it as security for a loan). Still, she lacked the funds to build the home. Seven years later, in 1903, she deeded the acreage to the African Methodist Episcopal Zion Church, an all-black congregation at which she had worshiped for years. The church built the home of Tubman's dreams in 1908. She was delighted to see the first residents move in, but she objected strenuously when the home's managers decided to charge an admission fee.

"When I gave the Home over to Zion Church," she told a local reporter, "what do you suppose they did? Why, they made a rule that nobody should come in without a hundred dollars. Now I wanted to make a rule that nobody could come in unless they had no money. What's the good of a Home if a person who wants to get in has to have money?" Tubman and the church finally reached a compromise, and in 1911, she moved into the home herself.

MOSES OF HER RACE ENDING HER LIFE IN HOME SHE FOUNDED read the headline of an article in the June 25, 1911, issue of the New York *World*. "She was the friend of great men," said the story, "but now, almost a centenarian, she awaits the last call. Now with the weight of almost a hundred years on her shoulders, she seeks rest during the few remaining days."

Tubman enjoyed more than a "few remaining days." Clear of mind, her always hearty appetite undiminished, she spent almost two years at the home, receiving visitors, telling stories, and, in late 1912, making out a will. (She left her house and its garden to a niece, a grandniece, and Frances Smith, the black woman who managed the home.) In February 1913, she chatted with an old friend, Mary B. Talbert, president of the New York State Federation of Colored Women's Clubs. Tubman, recalled Frances Smith, told Talbert "of the sweet spirit in that home, and of the happiness she felt was there." As Talbert prepared to leave, Tubman reached for her hand.

Holding it tightly, she expressed her hopes for the suffrage movement. "Tell the women," said Tubman, "to stand together."

A few weeks later, on March 10, 1913, Harriet Tubman died of pneumonia at the age of 93. Friends who had gathered at her bedside joined hands and sang her favorite spiritual, "Swing Low, Sweet Chariot."

Most of Auburn attended Tubman's last rites, a military service led by local Civil War veterans. As

In this photograph, probably the last ever taken of Tubman, the old fighter looks at the world with her usual unflinching gaze. As William Still had said so many years earlier, "Her like it is probable was never known before or since."

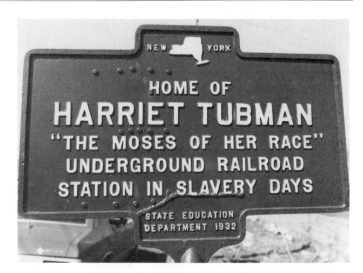

HOME OF
HARRIET TUBMAN
"THE MOSES OF HER RACE"
UNDERGROUND RAILROAD
STATION IN SLAVERY DAYS

STATE EDUCATION
DEPARTMENT 1932

Erected in 1932, an Auburn plaque boasts of one of the town's distinguished residents. Eighteen years earlier, almost everyone in Auburn had attended a memorial service for Tubman, who died at the age of 93. Blacks and whites, free citizens all, stood side by side as educator Booker T. Washington praised Tubman for bringing "the two races nearer together."

she was laid to rest, the old soldiers stood at crisp attention, mourners bowed their heads, a bugler played taps, and the flag of the United States snapped in the breeze. A year later, the town's citizens, black and white, took part in a memorial service for "the Moses of her race." The crowd listened intently as celebrated black educator Booker T. Washington spoke about the woman who had "brought the two races nearer together" and "made it possible for the white race to place a higher estimate upon the black race."

Harriet Tubman's dramatic work on the Underground Railroad has sometimes overshadowed her other accomplishments. She conducted hundreds of people to freedom; she was also a skilled military leader, a compassionate nurse, a tireless abolitionist, and a lifelong humanitarian. Carrying the scars of slavery through her long life, Tubman was willing to break the law when she believed it wrong. She stood by her people from start to finish.

Tubman never sought power, and she never had any. Uninterested in wealth, she remained poor all her life. Although she acquired scores of famous friends, she preferred to work quietly, shunning attention whenever she could. Of all the testimonials to this remarkable woman, perhaps the most incisive was delivered by Frederick Douglass in an 1868 letter to Tubman:

> The difference between us is very marked. Most that I have done and suffered in the service of our cause has been in public, and I have received much encouragement at every step of the way. You, on the other hand, have labored in a private way. I have wrought in the day—you in the night. I have had the applause of the crowd and the satisfaction that comes from being approved by the multitude, while the most that you have done has been witnessed by a few trembling, scarred, and foot-sore bondmen and women, whom you have led out of the house of bondage, and whose heartfelt "*God bless you*" has been your only reward. The midnight sky and the silent stars have been the witnesses of your devotion to freedom and of your heroism. Excepting John Brown—of sacred memory—I know of no one who has willingly encountered more perils and hardships to serve our enslaved people than you have. ❧

CHRONOLOGY

———— ⬥ ————

ca. 1820   Born Harriet Ross on the Brodas plantation in Dorchester County, Maryland

1827   Makes first attempt to escape from slavery

1835   Suffers a near-fatal blow to the head that leads to lifelong "sleeping fits"

1844   Marries John Tubman

1849   Escapes from slavery; befriends abolitionist leaders

1850   Makes first of 19 trips into the South as a conductor on the Underground Railroad

1852   Makes first trip to Canada

1857   Rescues parents from slavery; settles in Auburn, New York

1858   Meets abolitionist John Brown

1861   Travels to South Carolina to work with the Union army as a nurse

1863   Becomes a spy for the Union army; leads a raid on South Carolina's Combahee River; frees 750 slaves

1865   Works in Virginia hospital

1870   Marries Nelson Davis

1897   Receives a medal from Queen Victoria of England

1908   Builds a home for sick and elderly blacks

1911   Moves into home

1913   Dies of pneumonia

FURTHER READING

Aptheker, Herbert. *To Be Free: Studies in American Negro History.* New York: International Publishers, 1948.

Blockson, Charles L. *The Underground Railroad.* New York: Prentice-Hall, 1987.

Bradford, Sarah H. *Harriet Tubman: The Moses of Her People.* Secaucus, NJ: Citadel Press, 1974.

Campbell, Stanley W. *The Slave Catchers: Enforcement of the Fugitive Slave Law, 1850–1860.* Chapel Hill: University of North Carolina Press, 1968.

Conrad, Earl. *Harriet Tubman.* Washington, DC: Associated Publishers, 1942.

Duberman, Martin. *The Antislavery Vanguard: New Essays on the Abolitionists.* Princeton University Press, 1965.

Du Bois, W. E. B. *John Brown.* Philadelphia: Jacobs & Co., 1909.

Furnas, J. C. *Goodbye to Uncle Tom.* New York: William Sloane Associates, 1956.

Gara, Larry. *The Liberty Line: The Legend of the Underground Railroad.* Lexington: University of Kentucky Press, 1961.

McPherson, James M. *Battle Cry of Freedom.* New York: Oxford University Press, 1988.

Morris, Thomas D. *Free Men All: The Personal Liberty Laws of the North.* Baltimore: Johns Hopkins University Press, 1974.

Petry, Ann. *Harriet Tubman, Conductor on the Underground Railroad.* New York: Crowell, 1955.

Scott, John Anthony. *Hard Trials on My Way: Slavery and the Struggle Against It.* New York: Knopf, 1974.

INDEX

PICTURE CREDITS

M. W. TAYLOR is the former editor of the *New York Times* and *Los Angeles Times* syndicates and also served as an editor at *Life* magazine. Currently a New York City–based book editor and writer, she is coauthor of *Facts on File Dictionary of New Words*.

NATHAN IRVIN HUGGINS is W.E.B. Du Bois Professor of History and Director of the W.E.B. Du Bois Institute for Afro-American Research at Harvard University. He previously taught at Columbia University. Professor Huggins is the author of numerous books, including *Black Odyssey: The Afro-American Ordeal in Slavery*, *The Harlem Renaissance*, and *Slave and Citizen: The Life of Frederick Douglass*.